CHARACTERS

Miss Shepherd, about 65
Alan Bennett, the author's public persona
Alan Bennett 2, his inner persona
Mam, Alan Bennett's mother, 60s
Rufus, Alan Bennett's neighbour
Pauline, Rufus's wife
Social Worker, female
Underwood, a dilapidated figure
Mam's Doctor
Leo Fairchild, Miss Shepherd's brother
Lout
Ambulance Driver
Miss Shepherd's Doctor
Interviewer
Priest
Council workmen, Undertakers, etc.

The action of the play takes place in Alan Bennett's house
and garden and the street outside, in Camden, London

Time — 1974-1989

INTRODUCTION

After Miss Shepherd drove her van into my garden in 1974 friends used to ask me if I was planning to write a play about her. I wasn't, but twenty-five years later I have. There are plenty of reasons for the time-lag, the most obvious being that it would have been very difficult to write about her when she was alive and, as it were, on site.

"How can I write about her?" says one of the Alan Bennetts in the play. "She's *there*." And although the line was later cut it remains true.

Miss Shepherd's presence in the garden didn't, of course, stop me jotting things down, making notes on her activities and chronicling her various comic encounters. Indeed, in my bleaker moments it sometimes seemed that this was all there was to note down since nothing else was happening to me, hence, I suppose, the plaintive denials that make up the last speech in the play.

Still, there was no question of writing or publishing anything about her until she was dead or gone from the garden, and as time passed the two came to seem the same thing. Occasionally newspapers took an interest and tried to blow the situation up into a jolly news item, but again, as is said in the play, the ramparts of privacy were more impregnable in those pre-Murdoch days and she was generally left to herself. Even journalists who came to interview me were often too polite to ask what an (increasingly whiffy) old van was doing parked a few feet from my door. If they did enquire I would explain, while asking them to keep it to themselves, which they invariably did. I can't think that these days there would be similar discretion.

Miss Shepherd helped, of course, lying low if anybody came to my door, and at night straight away switching off her light whenever she heard a footstep. But though she was undoubtedly a recluse ("Is she", a neighbour once asked, "a genuine eccentric?"), Miss Shepherd was not averse to the occasional bout of celebrity. I came back one day to find her posing beside the van for a woman columnist (gender did count with Miss S.) who had somehow sweet-talked her into giving an interview, Miss Shepherd managing in the process to imply that I had over the years systematically stifled her voice. If she has since achieved any fame or notoriety through my having written about her, I suspect that she would think it no more than her due and that her position as writer of pamphlets and political commentator entitled her to public recognition or, as she says in the play, "the freedom of the land".

It was this imaginary celebrity — I think the psychological term for it is "delusion of reference" — that made her assume with every IRA bomb that she was next on the list. A disastrous fire in the Isle of Man meant, she was certain, that the culprit would now target her, and had she been alive at the time of Princess Diana's death she would have taken it as a personal warning to avoid travelling (in the van as distinct from a high-powered Mercedes) under the Pont d'Alma. In the first (and much longer) draft of the play this obsession was examined in more detail:

Miss Shepherd Mr Bennett. Will you look under the van?
Alan Bennett What for?
Miss Shepherd One of these explosive devices. There was another bomb last night and I think I may be the next on the list.
Alan Bennett Why you?
Miss Shepherd Because of Fidelis Party. The IRA may have got wind of it with a view to thwarting of reconciliation attempts, possibly. Look under the van.
Alan Bennett I can't see anything because of all your plastic bags.
Miss Shepherd Yes and the explosive's plastic so it wouldn't show, possibly. Are there any wires? The wireless tells you to look for wires. Nothing that looks like a timing device?
Alan Bennett There's an old biscuit tin.
Miss Shepherd No. That's not a bomb. It's just something that was on offer at Finefare. I ought to have special protection with being a party leader, increased risk through subverting of democracy, possibly.
Alan Bennett Nobody knows you're leader of a party.
Miss Shepherd Well, it was on an anonymous footing but somebody may have spilled the beans. No organization is watertight.

It's said of Robert Lowell that when he regularly went off his head it took the form of thinking he could rub shoulders with Beethoven, Voltaire and other all-time greats, with whom he considered himself to be on equal terms. (Actually Isaiah Berlin, about whose sanity there was no doubt, made exactly the same assumption but that's by the way). The Virgin Mary excepted, Miss Shepherd's sights were set rather lower. Her assumed equals were Harold Wilson, Mr Heath and (as she always called him) "Enoch" and I was constantly being badgered to find out their private addresses so that they could be sent the latest copy of *True View*. Atypically for someone unbalanced, Miss Shepherd never seemed to take much interest in the Royal Family, the Queen and the Duke of Edinburgh never thought of as potential readers. This did not mean, though, that she was a disloyal subject and on the occasion of the Queen's jubilee in 1977 there was only one flag to be seen in our well-to-do socialist street and that was in the back window of the van where only I could see it.

To begin with I wrote the play in three acts, knowing, though, that these days this is not a popular format. Still, that's how Miss Shepherd's story seemed to present itself, the first act consisting of her life in the street and culminating with her driving the van into the garden; the second act was life in the garden (all fifteen years of it), and the third act the events leading to her death and departure. The trouble with this way of telling the story was that whereas there was movement built into the first act (the lead-up to her arrival) and movement in the third (her decline and death), Act Two simply consisted of her being there, parked in the garden and going nowhere, the only movement me occasionally going up the wall. A second draft condensed the material into two acts, and though the passage of time within the play was perhaps not as clear, the passage of time within the theatre was altogether more acceptable, an hour each way quite enough for me. As Churchill said, the mind cannot take in more than the seat will endure.

Telling the truth crops up quite a bit in the play, what Miss Shepherd did or didn't do a subject of some disagreement between "the boys", as I tended to think of the two Alan Bennetts. They call not telling the truth "lying", but "the imagination" would be a kinder way of putting it, with Alan Bennett the writer finally winning through to make Miss Shepherd talk of her past (as she never actually did) and even to bring her back from the dead in order to take her bodily up to heaven (also imaginary). These departures from the facts were genuinely hard-won and took some coming to, causing me to reflect, not for the first time, that the biggest handicap for a writer is to have had a decent upbringing. Brought up not to lie or show off, I was temperamentally inclined to do both, particularly as a small child, and though reining me in perhaps improved my character it was no help in my future profession, where lying, or romancing anyway, is the essence of it. Nor did my education help. One of the difficulties I had in writing *The Madness of George III* was that, having been educated as a historian, I found it hard ever to take leave of the facts. With George III's first bout of madness the facts needed scarcely any alteration to make them dramatic and only a little tweaking was required, but even that I found hard to do. It was still harder to play around with the facts of Miss Shepherd's life, although the only person to know how much I may have doctored her history is me. And actually, while I've obviously had to compress a good deal, I haven't had to alter much at all. It's true, though, that a lengthier account of the events leading up to her moving into the garden with the van would make this development less dramatic, and less of a turning point.

What happened was that one night several of the van's windows were broken by two drunks, an incident that occurs in the play. This meant that Miss Shepherd was now much more at the mercy of the elements, the faded cretonne curtains which covered one or two of the windows her only protection from the weather and from prying eyes. I had a lean-to down some steps at the side of my house and now ran an electric lead out to this hut, so that on cold nights she could go in there to keep warm. Inevitably she began to spend the night there on a regular basis, the van becoming part office, part wardrobe, a repository for her pamphlets and her clothes and the place where she would spend what she saw as her working day. As I write I see Michael Frayn walking up the street *en route* from his home to his office nearby, where he writes. Miss Shepherd's routine was not very different, in this instance as in others mentioned in the play her life not as dissimilar from that of her neighbours as they would have liked to think. They had offices to go to and so did she. They had second homes and, having acquired a Robin Reliant, so did she, a parallel which Miss Ferris, the irritatingly patient (and somewhat jargon-ridden) social worker in the play, is not slow to point out. But with Miss Shepherd going to and from her sleeping quarters in the hut to her office in the van it meant that I got used to her crossing the garden in front of my window, so that when she did finally move in, bags and all, it was neither the surprise nor the life-changing decision (for both of us) that the play perhaps implies.

Over the years Miss Shepherd was visited by a succession of social workers, so Miss Ferris is a composite figure. To begin with the social workers got short shrift, their only function in Miss Shepherd's view to procure her concessions from the council: another walking stick, an additional wheelchair "in case this one conks out, possibly" and (a dream she never attained) the electrified chair in which she saw herself moving regally through the streets of Camden Town.

A composite, too, are the neighbours, Pauline and Rufus, though I have made Rufus a publisher in remembrance of my neighbour, the late Colin Haycraft, the proprietor of Duckworth's. Married to the novelist Alice Thomas Ellis, he regarded Miss Shepherd with a sceptical eye, never moderating his (not unpenetrating) voice when he was discussing her, though she might well be in the van only a few feet away. He, I'm sure, thought I was mad to let her stay. Still, he came to her funeral and as the coffin was slid into the hearse he remarked loudly as ever, "Well, it's a cut above her previous vehicle." Like Rufus in the play, Colin had little time for feminism. I once asked him if he was jealous of his wife's literary success. "Good God, no. One couldn't be jealous of a woman, surely?"

Though the character of Underwood is a fiction, invented in order to hint at something unexplained in Miss Shepherd's past (and ultimately to explain it), he had, certainly as regards his appearance, a basis in fact. When the van was still parked in the street the late Nicholas Tomalin and I had been mobilized by Miss Shepherd to push it forward a few yards to a fresh location. I wrote in my diary: "As we are poised for the move another Camden Town eccentric materializes, a tall, elderly figure in a long overcoat and Homburg hat with a distinguished grey moustache and in his buttonhole a flag for the Primrose League. Removing a grubby canary glove he leans a shaking hand against the rear of the van in a token gesture of assistance and when we have moved it the few statutory feet he puts the glove on again, saying grandly, 'If you should need me in the future I'm just around the corner' — i.e. in Arlington House."

For all the doubts I voice about tramps in the play, when one comes across such a fugitive from *Godot* it's hard not to think that Beckett's role as social observer has been underestimated.

I have allowed myself a little leeway in speculating about Miss Shepherd's concert career, though if, as her brother said, she had studied with Cortot she must have been a pianist of some ability. Cortot was the leading French pianist between the wars, Miss Shepherd presumably studying with him at the height of his fame. Continuing to give concerts throughout the Occupation, he finished the war under a cloud and it was perhaps this that sent him on a concert tour to England, where I remember seeing his photograph on posters sometime in the late forties. Perhaps Miss Shepherd saw it too, though by this time her hopes of a concert career must have been fading, a vocation as a nun already her goal.

Her war had been spent driving ambulances, a job for which she had presumably enlisted and been trained and which marked the beginning of her lifelong fascination with anything on wheels. Comically she figures in my mind alongside the Queen, who as Princess Elizabeth also did war service and as an ATS recruit was filmed in a famous piece of wartime propaganda changing the wheel on an army lorry, a vehicle my mother fondly believed HRH drove for the duration of hostilities.

What with land girls, nurses, Waafs, the ATS and Wrens, these were years of cheerful, confident, seemingly carefree women and I'd like to think of Miss Shepherd as briefly one of them, having the time of her life: accompanying a singsong in the NAAFI perhaps, snatching a meal in a British restaurant, then going to the pictures to see Leslie Howard or Joan Fontaine. It was maybe this taste of wartime independence that later unsuited her for the veil, or it may be, as her brother suggested, that she suffered shellshock after a bomb exploded near her ambulance. At any rate she was invalided out and this was when her troubles began, with, in her brother's view, the call of the convent a part of it.

I would have liked her concert career to have outlasted the war or to have resumed after the duration, when the notion of a woman playing the piano against psychological odds was the theme of the film *The Seventh Veil* (1945), with Ann Todd as the pianist Francesca and James Mason her tyrannical stick-wielding Svengali. Enormously popular at the time (and with it the Grieg Piano Concerto), the film set the tone for a generation of glamorous pianists, best known of whom was Eileen Joyce, who was reputed to change her frock between movements.

The Seventh Veil was subsequently adapted for the stage and I still have the programme of the matinee I saw at the Grand Theatre in Leeds in March

1951. The Grieg concerto had by this time been replaced by Rachmaninov Number 2 and James Mason by Leo Genn, but it was still Ann Todd, her guardian as ever bringing his stick down across her fingers as she cowered at the keyboard.

If Miss Shepherd had ever made it to the concert circuit this would be when I might have seen her, as I was by now going every week to symphony concerts in Leeds Town Hall where Miss Shepherd would have taken her place alongside Daphne Spottiswoode or Phyllis Sellick, Moura Lympany, Valda Aveling and Gina Bachauer — artistes with their décolletée, shawl-collared gowns as glamorous and imposing in my fourteen-year-old eyes as fashion models, Barbara Goalens of the keyboard, brought to their feet by the conductor to acknowledge the applause then sinking in a curtsy to receive the obligatory flowers, just as, in memory anyway, Miss Shepherd does in the play.

When I wrote the original account I glossed over the fact that Miss Shepherd's death occurred the same night that, washed and in clean things, she returned from the day centre. I chose not to make this plain because for Miss Shepherd to die then seemed so handy and convenient, just when a writer would (if a little obviously) have chosen for her to die. So I note that I was nervous not only of altering the facts to suit the drama but of even seeming to have altered them. But that night or in the early hours of the morning was when she did die, the nurse who took her to the day centre (who wasn't the social worker) saying that she had come across several cases when someone who had lived rough had seemed somehow to know that death was imminent and had made preparations accordingly, in Miss Shepherd's case not merely seeing that she was washed and made more presentable but the previous week struggling to confession and Mass.

A year or so earlier when Miss Shepherd had been ill I'd tried to get some help from what remained of the convent at the top of the street. I got nowhere but the visit confirmed me in my low opinion of nuns, or this particular order anyway. Another cut:

Alan Bennett 2 Nuns, it seems to me, took the wrong turning at the same time as British Rail. Around the time that porters were forced to forsake their black serge waistcoats, monkey jackets and oilcloth caps, so some monastic Dr Beeching decreed that nuns lose their billowing wimpled innocence and come on like prison wardresses in grey tricel twinsets.
Woman Yes?
Alan Bennett I live down the street.
Woman You do. I've seen you. It's you that has the van.
Alan Bennett Yes.
Woman Difficult woman.
Alan Bennett A Catholic.

Woman One of the sisters remembers her. You're not? Catholic.

Alan Bennett No.

Woman A novice. It may have been twice. Had two stabs at it. It takes a special type.

Alan Bennett 2 Cold brown lino on the floor, dimpled from being so often polished. Room spotless and uncomforting, the only ornament a crucifix.

Woman It's not an ornament at all.

Alan Bennett I've been told she was very argumentative.

Woman Disputatious she was. I've had her pointed out to me on that account. Chalking on the pavement and so on.

Alan Bennett That's all in the past. Did she play the piano?

Woman She did not. This is a house of God. There is no piano here. Anyway what is it you want?

Alan Bennett She's ill.

Woman Who? The woman?

Alan Bennett I wondered if there was a nun available who could talk to her, do her some shopping.

Woman We don't have shopping nuns. It's a strict order.

Alan Bennett I've seen them shopping. I saw one yesterday in Marks and Spencer. She was buying meringues.

Woman The Bishop may have been coming.

Alan Bennett Does he like meringues?

Woman What business is it of yours what the Monsignor likes? Who are you, coming round asking if the Bishop likes meringues? Are you a communist?

Alan Bennett I just thought there must be nuns with time on their hands.

Woman They don't have time on their hands. That's what prayer is for.

Alan Bennett But she's ill. She's a Catholic. I think she may be dying.

Woman They can pray for her, only you'll have to fill in a form. She'll probably pull her socks up once your back is turned. That's been my experience where invalids are concerned.

I make no apology for the fact that Miss Shepherd makes great play with place names: St Albans, Bodmin, Hounslow, Staines. Since the oddity of place names is a staple of English comedy I might be accused of introducing Dunstable, say, for an easy laugh. I was once taken to task by a critic for using Burgess Hill in a play, a name devoid of comic overtones for me but thought by the critic to be a sure indicator of my triviality of mind. I'd actually just been hard put to think of a place and asked the actor who had the line (it was Valentine Dyall) where he lived, hence Burgess Hill. But with Miss Shepherd the extended landscape of places she had known was very real to this now largely stationary wanderer and they were still vivid in her mind as the objects of journeys she was always planning (and sometimes threatening) to make.

When our paths first crossed in the late sixties there was much less dereliction on the streets of London than there is today. Camden Town had its resident company of tramps and eccentrics, it's true, by no means all of them homeless or beggars, but they were as an aristocracy compared with the dozens of young poor and homeless that nowadays sleep in its doorways and beg on the streets. Several of these ancient archetypal figures were long-time residents of Arlington House, among the last of the Rowton Houses that provided cheap accommodation for working men in London, the one in Camden Town still happily functioning today. Nowadays, though, the windows of its individual cubicles look across to spacious executive apartments and over the restaurants, clubs and all the tawdry chaos of Camden Lock, which to my mind is far more offensive and destructive of the area than the beggars have ever been.

Another speech cut from the play:

There is a community in dereliction even though it may not amount to much more than passing round a bottle. This seems especially apparent in Camden Town, where the doorway of the periodically defunct Odeon or the steps of the drop-in centre opposite are home to a band of social dysfuncts notable for their indiscriminate conviviality and sudden antipathies. Itinerant in that they periodically move on, or are made to do so, they do not go far, the premises of any enterprise that shows signs of faltering ("Shocking Discounts", "Everything Must Go") likely to be immediately roosted by this crew of slurred and contentious intoxicates.

Miss Shepherd, though, never thought of herself as a tramp. As a potential Prime Minister, how could she?

Alan Bennett 2 Our neighbourhood is peopled by several commanding widows and wives: there is Lady Pritchett, the wife of Sir Victor; there is Mrs Vaughan Williams, the widow of the composer, and occasionally to be seen is Elizabeth Jane Howard, the novelist and sometime wife of Kingsley Amis. All tall, grand roost-ruling women possessed of great self-confidence and assured of their position in the world. It is of this substantial sisterhood that Miss Shepherd sees herself as a natural member.

After Miss Shepherd died in April 1989 I had no immediate plans to write about her or any idea of the kind of thing I wanted to write but it was coming up to the tenth anniversary of the London Review of Books and I had promised Mary-Kay Wilmers that I would contribute something. So I put together an account of Miss Shepherd, using some of the material from my diaries and quoting from the pamphlets of hers that I had saved or rescued from the van. After this account had been published I had one or two stabs at turning it into a play but without success. Miss Shepherd's story was not difficult to tell; it was my own story over the same period that defeated me. Not that there was a great deal to be said, but somehow the two stories had to interconnect. It was only when I had the notion of splitting myself into two that the problem seemed to solve itself.

Still, very little of my own life is revealed, too little for one of the Alan Bennetts, who, having brought the play to a conclusion, breaks back to speak directly to the audience (a function he's previously left to his partner): "Look. This has been one path through my life — me and Miss Shepherd. Just one track. I wrote things; people used to come and stay the night, and of both sexes. What I mean to say is, it's not as if it's the whole picture. Lots of other stuff happened. No end of things."

The device of having two actors playing me isn't just a bit of theatrical showing off and does, however crudely, correspond to the reality. There was one bit of me (often irritated and resentful) that had to deal with this unwelcome guest camped literally on my doorstep, but there was another bit of me that was amused by how cross this eccentric lodger made me and that took pleasure in Miss Shepherd's absurdities and her outrageous demands.

There is no satisfactory way of dubbing these two parts (I would not call them halves) of my personality, and even if "the writer" would do for one, what is the other? The person? The householder? Or (a phrase from the courts) "the responsible adult"? As I wrote them first they were like an old married couple, complaining and finding fault with one another, nothing one thought or said a surprise to the other. I then started to find more fun in their relationship, made it teasing and even flirtatious, a line that the actors Nicholas Farrell and Kevin McNally made more of in rehearsal.

Alan Bennett the author then became definitely more mischievous, more amoral than the Alan Bennett who goes out dutifully in his Marigold gloves in order to scoop his unsavoury lodger's poop, so that in some sense the division between them illustrates Kafka's remark that to write is to do the devil's work. Of course Kafka doesn't imply the converse, that scooping the poop (or fetching Miss Shepherd her sherbet lemons) is God's work. I never felt it so and resented neighbours or well-wishers who cast me in the saintly role, preferring to be thought of as a fool. Still, there was no way of ducking these attributions of goodness, as the more I rebutted them the more selfless I seemed. "Kind is so tame," says Kevin McNally in the play and that at least comes from the heart.

In one particular instance, I wish the part of me Kevin McNally plays had in life been more venturesome. The cheap commercialization of Camden High Street was just getting into its stride in 1989 when Miss Shepherd died but it was already far enough advanced for fliers about new boutiques and cafés to be put regularly through my door. At that time I let slip several opportunities that someone of a more mischievous temper than mine might well have taken up. Being on the electoral roll, Miss Shepherd was sent as many circulars as I was, including several from restaurants offering a free dinner (generally candlelit) to potential customers. I didn't avail myself of any of these offers but I regret now that I didn't pass on her vouchers to Miss Shepherd, as I would quite like to have seen the scene in such a restaurant with Miss Shepherd scowling and slurping (and smelling), surrounded by the appalled residents of Primrose Hill.

We were fortunate with the play to have a long rehearsal period (five and a half weeks) plus two weeks of previews, a time in which the anticipated difficulties of getting the van on to the stage and hoisting it off could be dealt with. In the event there were few problems with the van or the Robin Reliant, which also does a tour of the stage. What took up the time was the text, in particular the presentation of the two selves. Should they be dressed alike, for instance, in sports coat, M&S corduroys, suede shoes, the clothes I like to think I just happened to be wearing when the designer, Mark Thompson, paid me a visit, but near enough, I suppose, to what I wear every day? But are these the proper garments of my inner voice? Should the other self be put into something more sophisticated and metropolitan, black trousers, perhaps, a black polo neck?

In the end we decided that would be simplistic and so the two selves were dressed alike, and though this means that some of the audience are a bit slow to understand what is going on, it is probably better and sillier (which I like) to make them Tweedledum and Tweedledee. They were luckier than Maggie Smith, who as Miss Shepherd had to deck herself out in a variety of outfits, many of them quick changes, which had to be achieved in the cramped interior of the van.

Over the years Miss Shepherd had four or five vans, of which in the stage production we see two: the one (donated by Lady Wiggin) which she drives on to the stage half-way through the first act, and another, supposedly the same, on which the curtain rises for Act II, but since this is several years later now transformed by Miss Shepherd's usual coat of scrambled egg or badly made custard. Miss Shepherd's fascination with any aid to locomotion meant that she over-supplied herself not only with vans but even with walking sticks, of which she had many, one of which Maggie Smith uses in the play. It still bears traces of Miss Shepherd's characteristic yellow paint, evidence of her last painting job done on the three-wheeler which she parked outside my gate, where (another relic) the kerb still shows a few tell-tale yellow spots.

The three-wheeler had a predecessor, a battered Mini, but this was stolen only a month or two after Miss Shepherd acquired it and it was later found abandoned in the basement of the council flats in Maiden Lane near King's Cross. Like the Reliant, its chief function had been as a supplementary wardrobe and it was thus heavily pervaded by Miss Shepherd's characteristic odour. I felt slightly sorry for the thieves (who were never, of course, caught), imagining them making off with the vehicle and only as they sped illicitly through Camden Town being hit by the awfulness of what it contained, this realization signalled by expressions of vernacular fastidiousness such as "Do me a favour!", "Cor, strike a light!" or, as the scent took hold, "Jesus wept!" So that when, having gone to Maiden Lane to recover some of her papers from the car, I found it bearing a Police Aware notice, I felt that it had, in this case, a heightened significance.

I have always spelled her name Shepherd but I think the correct spelling, if an assumed name can have a correct spelling, was Sheppard, the difference, I suppose, distinguishing between the character whom I knew and the one I have written about. At one early stage, out of a courtesy which was probably even then old-fashioned, I called her Mrs Shepherd, a designation which she did not immediately correct. Nowadays, of course, such delicacy seems misplaced, and also fanciful, because if she was Mrs Shepherd there must have been a Mr Shepherd and he would be very hard to imagine.

Miss Shepherd was solipsistic to a degree, and in her persistent refusal to take into account the concerns or feelings of anyone else except herself and her inability to see the world and what happened in it except as it affected her, she behaved more like a man than a woman. I took this undeviating selfishness to have something to do with staying alive. Gratitude, humility, forgiveness or fellow feelings were foreign to her nature or had become so over the years, but had she been otherwise she might not have survived as long as she did. She hated noise, though she made plenty, particularly when sitting in her three-wheeler on a Sunday morning revving the engine to recharge the battery. She hated children. Reluctant to have the police called when the van's window had been broken and herself hurt, she would want the law summoning if there were children playing in the street and making what she considered too much noise or indeed any noise at all.

She inhabited a different world from ordinary humanity, a world in which the Virgin Mary could be encountered outside the Post Office in Parkway and Mr Khrushchev higher up the street; a world in which her advice was welcomed by world leaders and the College of Cardinals took note of her opinion. Seeing herself as the centre of this world, she had great faith in the power of the individual voice, even though it could only be heard through pamphlets photocopied at Prontaprint or read on the pavement outside Williams and Glyn's Bank.

Though I never questioned Miss Shepherd on the subject, what intrigued me about the regular appearances put in by the Virgin Mary was that she seldom turned up in her traditional habiliments; no sky-blue veil for her, still less a halo. Before leaving heaven for earth the BVM always seemed to go through the dressing-up box so that she could come down as Queen Victoria, say, or dressed in what sounded very much like a sari. And not only her. One of my father's posthumous appearances was as a Victorian statesman and an old tramp, grey-haired and not undistinguished, was confidently identified as St Joseph (though minus his donkey), just as I was taken briefly for St John.

With their fancy dress and a good deal of gliding about, it was hard not to find Miss Shepherd's visions comic, but they were evidence of a faith that manifestly sustained her and a component of her daily and difficult life. In one of her pamphlets she mentions the poet Francis Thompson, who was as Catholic as she was (and who lived in similar squalor). Her vision of the intermingling of this world and the next was not unlike his:

> But (when so sad thou canst not sadder)
> Cry: — and upon thy so sore loss
> Shall shine the traffic of Jacob's ladder
> Pitched betwixt Heaven and Charing Cross.
> Yea, in the night, my Soul, my daughter,
> Cry, — clinging Heaven by the hems;
> And lo, Christ walking on the water
> Not of Gennesareth, but Thames!

It's now ten years since Miss Shepherd died, but hearing a van door slide shut will still take me back to the time when she was in the garden. For Marcel, the narrator in Proust's *Remembrance of Things Past,* the sound that took him back was that of the gate of his aunt's idyllic garden; with me it's the door of a broken-down Commer van. The discrepancy is depressing but then most writers discover quite early on that they're not going to be Proust. Besides, I couldn't have heard my own garden gate because in order to deaden the (to her) irritating noise Miss Shepherd had insisted on me putting a piece of chewing gum on the latch.

This is the third of my plays to have been directed by Nicholas Hytner and designed by Mark Thompson and I am, as ever, greatly in their debt. Without Nicholas Hytner's encouragement and his help with the text the play could not have been staged; he is an ideal collaborator and all any playwright could want in a director.

I would like to thank the cast, too, for their help in shaping and animating the text, particularly, of course, Maggie Smith, who brought Miss Shepherd to the stage and whose wit, perception and sheer fun made the play a joy to do.

A. B.

AUTHOR'S NOTES

Music

The hymn sung by the novices at the start of the play should be familiar and common to both Catholic and Anglican congregations and, if possible, Nonconformist congregations too, thus giving it the widest possible appeal. In this production we used *As Pants the Hart* (Tune: All Saints) partly because it was familiar but also because the notion of a chase seemed apt.

The piano music which is repeated at various points in the play was originally intended to be Schubert's Andante in B Flat Major but this was perhaps too lyrical and we ended up using Beethoven's Piano Sonata No 27, Opus 90 in E Minor. The piano climax which ends Act I was also Beethoven, the end of Piano Sonata No. 23, Opus 57, the "Apassionata".

When Miss Shepherd is praying and the van takes on its unearthly aspect it was accompanied by faint spectral bells and when it gloriously ascends into heaven at the end of Act II it does so to Richard Sisson's celestial choir.

The Vehicles

I am not sure how many vans Miss Shepherd had in the time that I knew her, but it was at least three and possibly five. In the play there are three vans, only two of which are actually seen. The first unseen vehicle is the one Miss Shepherd asks Alan Bennett to push down Albany Street at the start of the play and which she subsequently parks in his street. For the purposes of the action this is taken to be off stage left. Half-way through Act I this van is removed by the council and it is its replacement, still in its original trim, that is driven on to the stage by Miss Shepherd and parked, as it were, in Alan Bennett's garden.

It is still there when the curtain rises on Act II, but by now it is painted Miss Shepherd's favourite scrambled-egg yellow. This in practical terms means that during the interval the first-act van has to be switched for an identical one painted in yellow. It is this switch which necessitates the use of a front cloth, because otherwise some element of surprise would be lost. And, of course, it's not only that the van has been painted yellow; it's also been festooned with odd bits of carpet and the underneath stuffed with bulging plastic bags, all of which have accumulated over the years.

Not long into Act II, Miss Shepherd drives her Robin Reliant on to the stage. This too is in its original trim and when she reverses it off stage it's again notionally parked in the street off stage left, where she spends a good deal of time painting it and revving it up. This revving up, which was generally done on a Sunday morning, was intended to recharge the battery. I thought it useless as I was under the impression the wheels had to go round before the battery was charged. I said as much in the book of *The Lady in the Van*, and then had shoals of letters pointing out what a fool I was. So Miss Shepherd had the last laugh there too.

The van was parked laterally across the stage with the bonnet stage centre so that facing the audience was the sliding door through which the audience got a glimpse of its festering interior. However, in the interludes when we see Miss Shepherd at prayer, which if not magical are at least unearthly, the van slowly revolved so that the bonnet was upstage and the rear doors faced the audience. These double doors then magically (and silently) opened to reveal Miss Shepherd at her devotions. I had hoped that we could have taken this magical element even further and split the van to form some kind of diptych, but if it could have been done it would have been ruinously expensive and (I tell myself) might not have worked.

Staging
Scenes are generally quite short and flow into one another. Scenes occasionally begin with a slight pause (as in the social worker's first meeting with Alan Bennett), the pause indicating that a question (which the audience knows is coming) has already been asked. One critic complained that this was a revue-style format, as if it were something I had overlooked rather than made a feature of the play's construction. One sighs but goes on: a critic made exactly the same criticism of my first play more than thirty years ago.

There are no doors or doorbells, so that when Miss Shepherd comes into the house or over to the desk she does not waste time by ringing the bell but walks straight in. This is a stage convention but it is not unlike Miss Shepherd's usual behaviour when, though she had to ring the bell, she would try if she could not to linger on the doorstep ("I can't stand the noise. I'm a sick woman.") but slip past me into the hall and sit on the stairs.

Alan Bennett is played by two actors, Alan Bennett, who takes part in the action, and Alan Bennett 2, who describes and comments on it. They are dressed identically (sports coat, shirt, plain coloured tie, grey pullover and corduroy trousers with suede shoes) and though the play covers a period of twenty years during which there were some startling changes in fashion (flares, for instance), these changes are not reflected in the Alan Bennetts, who remain the same throughout. This too, I have to admit, is not just a production device but a fair reflection of the facts.

To establish the difference in their roles Alan Bennett 2 should, to begin with at any rate, remain tethered to his desk so that his function as writer and observer is made plain. He is taken to be invisible to the other characters, nor does he talk, except to himself, as it were, and to the audience. It's only after Miss Shepherd dies that he becomes visible to her and available for conversation, whereupon, true to form, she plays him off against his other self.

A.B.

Other plays by Alan Bennett published by Samuel French Ltd:

Enjoy

Getting On

Habeas Corpus

Kafka's Dick (revised)

Office Suite:
Green Forms *and* A Visit from Miss Protheroe

The Old Country

Say Something Happened

Single Spies:
An Englishman Abroad *and* A Question of Attribution

Talking Heads:
Bed Among the Lentils
A Chip in the Sugar
A Cream Cracker Under the Settee
Her Big Chance
A Lady of Letters
Soldiering On
A Woman of No Importance

The Wind in the Willows

ACT I

Alan Bennett's house and garden, Camden, London

The play is set on an open stage. Permanently onstage, DR, there is a desk with a chair and a lamp, and also an easy chair. During the play scenery is flown in from time to time to represent the street and the interior of the house, though not altogether naturalistically

When the CURTAIN rises, a front cloth masks the stage, with, inset, the bay window of an early nineteenth-century house. The forestage and the window are lit. To the L of the desk area is the street. Miss Shepherd, at this point resembling a bundle of old coats, lies here. She is tall and though her changes of costume will not be described in detail, she is generally dressed in an assortment of coats and headscarves but with a variety of other hats superimposed on the headscarves. Old raincoats figure, as do carpet slippers and skirts which have often been lengthened by the simple process of sewing on additional strips of material. She is about sixty-five

A hymn begins, sung by a chorus of young girls

Alan Bennett 2 looks through the window briefly then disappears from view, sitting at the desk

The hymn is cut off abruptly and the front cloth rises to reveal Alan Bennett 2; Alan Bennett is on stage, in the desk area, but as yet not discernible. The Lights come up in the desk area and the street

During the following speech, Miss Shepherd slowly gets to her feet

Alan Bennett 2 (*reading from what he has been writing*) The smell is sweet, with urine only a minor component, the prevalent odour suggesting the inside of someone's ear. Dank clothes are there too, wet wool and onions, which she eats raw, plus what for me has always been the essence of poverty, damp newspaper. Miss Shepherd's multi-flavoured aroma is masked by a liberal application of various talcum powders, with Yardley's Lavender always a favourite, and when she is sitting down it is this genteel fragrance that dominates, the second subject, as it were, in her odoriferous concerto. It is only when she rises that the original theme returns, the terrible primary odour now triumphantly restated and left to hang in the room long after she has departed.

Miss Shepherd I'm by nature a very clean person. I have a testimonial for a Clean Room, awarded me some years ago, and my aunt, herself spotless, said I was the cleanest of my mother's children, particularly in the unseen places.

Alan Bennett 2 Having builders in the house means that I am more conscious of the situation so I determine to speak out.

Alan Bennett moves from the desk area to Miss Shepherd

Alan Bennett Miss Shepherd. There is a strong smell of urine.

Miss Shepherd Well, what do you expect when they're raining bricks down on me all day? And then I think I've got a mouse, so that would make for a cheesy smell, possibly.

The Lights go down on Miss Shepherd

Mam, Alan Bennett's mother, also in her sixties, enters R

Mam Alan. Can I ask you a question?

Alan Bennett The answer is, I've no idea.

Mam You don't know the question yet.

Alan Bennett I do know the question. The question is, where does she go to the lav?

Alan Bennett 2 Lavatories always loom large with my mother. What memory was to Proust the lavatory is to my mam.

Mam Well, where?

Alan Bennett The answer is, I don't know.

Mam You don't know, with that smell? Well, I know, and I haven't been to Oxford. Her knickers. She does it in her britches.

The Lights change

Mam exits

Alan Bennett 2 Cut to five years earlier. I am standing by the convent in Camden Town looking up at the crucifix on the wall, trying to decide what's odd about it. Normally when Jesus is on the cross he looks — well, relaxed. (Nothing more he can do about it, after all.) Here he looks tense, on edge — it's as if he's escaped through one of the barred windows and flattened himself on the cross in order to avoid the German searchlights. He's the Christ of Colditz.

Miss Shepherd You're looking up at the cross. You're not St John, are you?

Alan Bennett St John who?

Miss Shepherd St John. The disciple whom Jesus loved.

Alan Bennett No. My name's Bennett.

Miss Shepherd Well, if you're not St John I want a push for the van. It conked out, the battery possibly. I put some water in only it hasn't done the trick.

Alan Bennett Was it distilled water?

Miss Shepherd It was holy water so it doesn't matter if it was distilled or not. The oil is another possibility.

Alan Bennett That's not holy too?

Miss Shepherd Holy oil in a van? Don't be silly. It would be far too expensive. I want pushing to Albany Street.

Alan Bennett 2 Scarcely have I put my shoulder to the back of the van, an old Bedford, than in textbook fashion Miss Shepherd goes through her repertory of hand signals: "I am moving off — I am turning left" — the movements done with such boneless grace this section of the Highway Code might have been choreographed by Balanchine with Ulanova at the wheel.

Miss Shepherd What have we stopped for?

Alan Bennett This is Albany Street.

Miss Shepherd The top of Albany Street. I want the bottom.

Alan Bennett That's a mile away.

Miss Shepherd So? You're young. I'm in dire need of assistance. I'm a sick woman, dying possibly.

Alan Bennett It's too far.

Miss Shepherd You're wicked.

Alan Bennett You thought I was St John.

Miss Shepherd Anybody can make a mistake. I like to keep a low profile. I don't want to take the eye of the police through being stationary on the carriageway.

Alan Bennett You can park anywhere.

Alan Bennett 2 Which you could of course in those unpenalized days.

Miss Shepherd Where do *you* live?

Alan Bennett Just along the road.

Miss Shepherd I could park there.

Alan Bennett I'll help push you down Albany Street.

Miss Shepherd and Alan Bennett exit

During the following, Alan Bennett enters and goes to the desk area

Alan Bennett 2 And out of my life, I thought. Were I a proper writer I would welcome such an encounter as constituting experience, but I have no curiosity. True, I have started noting down the odd things people say, but contact with the actual creatures themselves I keep to a minimum. Meanwhile I seem to be buying a house.

Rufus and Pauline, Alan Bennett's neighbours, enter and move into the desk area

Rufus It's a pretty house, smaller than ours, of course, but you're unattached.
Alan Bennett No. It's attached to the house next door.
Rufus No, I meant you. You're — single.
Alan Bennett Oh yes. Yes.
Rufus Sickert once lived in the street, apparently; Dickens's abandoned wife and in one of the houses I believe someone was murdered. Now it's the usual north London medley: advertising, journalism, TV, the odd architect ... Dare one ask how much?
Alan Bennett Well, there's no back garden.
Pauline We do have a back garden. And a front, of course.
Rufus *Cuanta costa?*
Alan Bennett Eleven thousand five hundred pounds.
Rufus Oh my God!
Alan Bennett I know.
Rufus Such a shame you've had to come in at the top of the market. And of course what I'm thinking is we're opposite. So what is the value of our own little abode?
Pauline (*happily*) Sad.
Rufus Call me a socialist if you like, but I think that accommodation (which is what a house is, after all) ought to be within the reach of all classes in the country. I feel sorry for young people.
Pauline I feel sorry for old people, too.
Alan Bennett At least I can fetch my car in.
Rufus We've had a run-in made for ours. That will have upped the value again. Tragic.
Alan Bennett The van at the top.
Rufus The woman? Yes, she seems to have settled outside number forty-two.
Alan Bennett Do they mind?
Rufus I hope not. I like to think this is a community.

The Lights cross-fade to the street, L

Rufus and Pauline exit

During the following, Alan Bennett moves into the street

Miss Shepherd enters L

Miss Shepherd gives Alan Bennett a pamphlet and he gives her a coin

Alan Bennett 2 The woman in the van sells pamphlets. I came across her today outside Williams and Glyn's Bank on the corner of Camden High Street. She'd chalked a picture of St Francis on the pavement. At least I took it to be St Francis ... the cowled figure actually looked like Red Riding Hood; only one or two birds winging in for a bit of conversation gave the game away.

Alan Bennett reads the pamphlet

Miss Shepherd I also sell pencils. They only cost a copper but a gentleman came by the other day and said that the pencil he had bought from me was the best pencil on the market at the present time. It lasted him three months. He'll be back for another shortly.
Alan Bennett You're against the Common Market, I see.
Miss Shepherd Not me. The soul in question.
Alan Bennett You're not the writer?
Miss Shepherd Not necessarily. I'll go so far as to say this. They are anonymous. And they are a shilling. You only gave me a sixpence.
Alan Bennett It says in the pamphlet St Francis hurled money from him.
Miss Shepherd Yes, but he was a saint. He could afford to.
Alan Bennett 2 (*taking the pamphlet from Alan Bennett*) Can I have that?
Alan Bennett Why? Are you going to save it?
Alan Bennett 2 It might come in handy.

The Lights fade on the street setting and the Alan Bennetts return to the desk area

Pauline enters

Pauline Can you watch the house? Keys are in here. (*She gives Alan Bennett an envelope*) I hear madam's been given the push from forty-two. She's getting nearer. Outside number seventy now. Still, they've got a son at Bedales and the daughter's a cello fanatic; they'll probably like her.
Alan Bennett Mrs Vaughan Williams says her name is Shepherd. Been a nun at some point.
Pauline Can you watch the house? We're off to foreign parts. France.
Alan Bennett I didn't know you could be an ex-nun. I thought once you'd signed on it was quite hard to kick the habit. Anywhere in particular? In France?

Pauline No. We just let the trusty Volvo follow its nose. Wayfarers all!

Pauline exits

Mam enters L and sits on a chair. A Light comes up on her

Alan Bennett 2 My mother is on the phone.
Mam I wish I was good.
Alan Bennett You are good.
Mam No, the way other people are good.
Alan Bennett Where are you sitting?
Mam On a chair in the passage.
Alan Bennett 2 That's how her depressions always start, sitting on an unaccustomed chair. The doctor's put her on tablets.
Alan Bennett They won't work. They never do.

Alan Bennett 2 pays no attention, but looks out of the window, up the street

We're on the hospital trail again.

There comes the sound of the van starting up, off

The Light goes down on Mam and she exits

Oh God, she's on the move.
Alan Bennett 2 And out comes the undulating greasy-raincoated arm to indicate "I am moving off."
Alan Bennett Whose turn will it be now?
Alan Bennett 2 Mrs Vaughan-Williams?
Alan Bennett No. Not the Birts?
Alan Bennett 2 Fifty-eight?
Alan Bennett No.
Alan Bennett 2 "I am coming to a halt."
Alan Bennett No! Not there. She can't park there. What will I tell them? I'm supposed to be watching the house.

Miss Shepherd enters L and moves to the desk area

Miss Shepherd I want a ruler. A tape measure would do. I must measure the distance between the tyres and the kerb.
Alan Bennett What for?
Miss Shepherd One and a half inches is the ideal gap. There needs to be proper circulation of air or decay might set in. I came across it once in a

Catholic motoring magazine under tips on Christian parking. The tyres are sacred tyres. They haven't been pumped up since 1964. Still, that doesn't mean one should dispense with the necessary precautions.

Alan Bennett I'm not sure you should park there at all. They're away in France.

Miss Shepherd On pilgrimage?

Alan Bennett No.

Miss Shepherd I went on pilgrimage once, not long after the war. Slept on the floor in a church hall.

Alan Bennett You didn't stay long outside number fifty.

Miss Shepherd Because it was non-stop music. I had to ring the bell. The daughter said something about her A-levels. I said it's the noise levels I'm worried about. I'd seen him with an umbrella, I thought they were a nice family.

Alan Bennett 2 Ask her. Ask her how long she's been in the van.

Alan Bennett How long have you been living in the van?

Miss Shepherd Who says I live there? I may spend the night there on occasion but it's only a *pied-à-terre.*

Alan Bennett Where do you live?

Miss Shepherd I got it to put my things in, though don't spread that around. I came down from St Albans and plan to go back there in due course. I'm just pedalling water at the moment but I've always been in the transport line. I drove ambulances in the war. I've got good topography. I knew Kensington in the black-out.

Mr Bennett. They're not musical, are they?

Alan Bennett Who?

Miss Shepherd Opposite. Sixty-two.

Alan Bennett No. Though they go to the opera. What happened to "Hallo? Goodbye?"

Miss Shepherd exits

Alan Bennett 2 Well, she's "a sick woman, dying possibly."

The Lights cross-fade to the street

Rufus and Pauline enter L

Alan Bennett meets them

Alan Bennett I was out when she moved down. I came back and there she was. Do you mind?

Rufus Mind? My dear man! Why should we mind? We can only be grateful you didn't land us with squatters. Ha ha.

Alan Bennett returns to the desk area

Pauline People have to live somewhere.
Rufus Not outside our gate.
Pauline We can't move her on.
Rufus Why? Everyone else has.
Pauline She's as much right to be here as we have.
Rufus No she hasn't. Still, I suppose we shan't be here for ever. I see this as just the first rung on the ladder.
Pauline Alan says she's apparently trying to get back to St Albans. It's like that man in *The Caretaker*, trying to get back to Sidcup.
Rufus What caretaker?
Pauline Pinter. He's trying to get back to Sidcup. She's trying to get back to St Albans.
Rufus Well, maybe she could park outside his house?
Pauline Who?
Rufus Pinter.

The Lights cross-fade back to the desk area

Pauline and Rufus exit

Alan Bennett 2 I can't work. And the van doesn't help. When I can't work I watch her.
Alan Bennett So write it down.
Alan Bennett 2 No. I write about one old woman as it is. Mam. The last thing I want to do is write about another. Besides, tramps these days need to be taken with a pinch of salt. Godot has a lot to answer for. With their gnomic wisdom and obligatory truth-telling, the vagabond these days is rather overdone, the threadbare somewhat threadbare.

An Interviewer enters the desk area

Interviewer What was your first play about?
Alan Bennett Public school.
Interviewer But you didn't go to public school.
Alan Bennett No, but I read about it.
Interviewer And what's your next play about?
Alan Bennett Sex. I read about that too.
Interviewer Do you like living on your own?
Alan Bennett It's always women who put that question. Men don't even bother to ask.

Interviewer Have you never lived with anybody?

Alan Bennett My parents.

Alan Bennett 2 This is 1971, when the ramparts of privacy were more impregnable than they are now. So this "anybody" I have never lived with remains unsexed, a shadowy figure with the focus never sharp enough to reveal whether it is decked out in trousers or frock.

Alan Bennett I doubt that the house will ever ring with the sound of childish laughter. Other than mine, of course.

Interviewer Oh, incidentally, does someone actually live in that van across the street? I saw a woman getting in.

Alan Bennett What van? (*He looks*) *I* don't know. I've never noticed it before.

The Interviewer exits

(*To Alan Bennett 2*) She's a journalist. She'd only have written about her. I thought you were wanting to do that.

Alan Bennett 2 No fear.

Alan Bennett You make notes.

Alan Bennett 2 Only as a diary. And on the Everest principle. She's there.

The Lights change; the area L is now the garden

Suddenly all hell breaks loose; we hear the sound of banging on the side of the van, off

Alan Bennett (*calling*) Yes? Can I help you?

A Man enters the garden

Man No. Why?

Alan Bennett (*moving into the garden*) What the fuck do you think you're doing? An old lady lives there.

Man I know that. What do you think I'm banging for? I want to have a look at her, don't I?

Alan Bennett Why?

Man Why not? You still on the telly then? You're nervous. You're trembling all over. Fucking cunt.

The Man exits

Miss Shepherd appears, but not from the direction of the van

Alan Bennett I thought you were in the van.

Miss Shepherd No, I was in the terrace, on the pavement. The air's better there.

Alan Bennett Somebody's been banging on the side of the van.

Miss Shepherd Oh yes? What did he want?

Alan Bennett I don't know what he wanted. Thumping, probably.

Miss Shepherd He wasn't a Catholic gentleman of refined appearance?

Alan Bennett No. He was a lout.

Miss Shepherd He may have been wanting a pencil. Or a pamphlet possibly. When you provide a service you do get these callers.

Alan Bennett Miss Shepherd. This was a hooligan.

Miss Shepherd Some people might say I was a tramp. It's just want of perception. You rub people up the wrong way. You should be like me, take people as they come.

A female Social Worker enters carrying a bag of clothes

Alan Bennett goes back to the desk area

Social Worker Miss Shepherd. I'm Jane, the social worker.

Miss Shepherd I don't want the social worker. I'm about to listen to *Any Answers*.

Social Worker I've brought you some clothes. You wrote asking for a coat.

Miss Shepherd Not during *Any Answers*. I'm a busy woman. I only asked for one coat.

Social Worker I brought three, in the event you fancied a change.

Miss Shepherd Where am I supposed to put three coats? Besides, I was planning on washing this coat in the not too distant future, so that makes four. My wardrobe's driving me mad.

Social Worker This is my old nursing mac.

Miss Shepherd I have a mac. Besides, green isn't my colour. Have you got a stick?

Social Worker The council have that in hand. It's been precepted for.

Miss Shepherd Will it be long enough?

Social Worker Yes. It's one of our special sticks.

Miss Shepherd I don't want a special stick. I want an ordinary stick. Only longer. Does it have one of those rubber things on it?

Social Worker I imagine so.

Miss Shepherd It has to have a rubber thing. It's no earthly use to me without the rubber thing, as you'd know if you weren't so young. I hope you're bona fide. You have a look of someone foreign.

Social Worker I'm just new. Is it all right if I call from time to time?

Miss Shepherd Not during *Any Answers*. And *Petticoat Line* is another programme I tune in for. They'll sometimes have discussion on the Common Market from a woman's point of view.

Social Worker If I should want to get in touch with you whom should I call?

Miss Shepherd I don't want to be got in touch with.

Social Worker There must be someone.

Miss Shepherd You can try Mr Bennett, only don't take any notice of what he says. He's a communist, possibly.

Alan Bennett returns to the garden and the Social Worker turns to him

Alan Bennett Me? Did you ask the people opposite? They're nearer.

Social Worker They said they didn't relate to her. You were the one she related to.

A Bennett Is that what they said — "related to"?

Social Worker No. That's me. They said you were her pal. She was your girlfriend. They didn't mean that, obviously.

Alan Bennett No.

The Social Worker exits

(*To Miss Shepherd*) She seemed very understanding, the social worker.

Miss Shepherd Not understanding enough. I ask for a wheelchair and what does she get me? A walking stick. It doesn't matter. I may be going soon.

Alan Bennett Where to?

Miss Shepherd Bodmin possibly. Or Hounslow. I'm undecided. Mr Bennett. I saw a snake this afternoon. It was coming up Parkway. It was a long grey snake, a boa constrictor possibly; it looked poisonous. It was keeping close to the wall and seemed to know the way. It looked as if it might be heading for the van. Mr Bennett, I thought I'd better tell you, just to be on the safe side. I've had some close shaves with snakes.

Alan Bennett 2 I do not believe in the snake, let alone the purposeful glint in its eye, but I do not say so, and when I find the next day that there has been a break-in at the pet shop in Parkway so there may have been a snake on the run, I feel some remorse.

Visiting my mother, I find her depression has deepened, bringing with it delusions.

Mam enters

Mam Alan.

Alan Bennett What?

Mam Come down here.
Alan Bennett What for?
Mam There's some massive birds on the wall.
Alan Bennett There never are. There's nothing on the wall. You're imagining things.
Mam There are. There are.

Mam exits

Alan Bennett 2 And there were, lined up on the garden wall, four peacocks from the hall. So, boa constrictors in the street, peacocks on the wall, it seems that both at the northern and southern gates of my life stands a deluded woman.
Alan Bennett Except you just said they aren't.
Alan Bennett 2 Aren't what?
Alan Bennett Deluded.
Alan Bennett 2 Well, not in this particular instance.
Alan Bennett And they're not the same, Mam and Miss Shepherd.
Alan Bennett 2 No, Alan, they are not. But they are both old ladies. So who better fearlessly to chronicle their intrepid lives than me? That appears to be my niche, apparently. Old ladies are my bread and butter.

The Lights fade to a night-time setting. There is the sound of breaking glass

Miss Shepherd enters

Alan Bennett moves into the garden

Miss Shepherd It was two young men. They may have been the worse for drink, by mistake. That does occur through not having eaten, possibly. I don't want a case.
Alan Bennett But your cheek's cut. I ought to call the police.
Miss Shepherd No, I don't want that. I don't want the police.
Alan Bennett Are you sure? You're bleeding.
Miss Shepherd I had a curry last week from the Taj Mahal and there's a bit of onion left. If I put it on in poultice form that should do the trick. Have you heard anything of Mr Khrushchev recently?
Alan Bennett No.
Miss Shepherd He hasn't disappeared from Russia?
Alan Bennett I don't think so. Why?
Miss Shepherd I saw him in Parkway this afternoon, him and another feller, a bit on the ginger side with braces. I'm wondering if he's been kidnapped. Perhaps you could just telephone the police, tell them about the windows then in passing as it were, I could steer it round to Mr Khrushchev.

Alan Bennett Let's leave it, shall we?

Miss Shepherd You were all for calling the police a minute or two ago and now you've gone off it. Do you know what your trouble is? You can't make up your mind.

The Lights change to a daytime setting L

Miss Shepherd exits

Pauline and Rufus enter

Pauline You should have called the police.

Alan Bennett Why? They're no better. I woke up at five the other morning and there's two of them idly shining their torches in the windows, hoping she'll wake up and enliven a dull hour of their beat.

Rufus I'd like to shove red-hot knitting needles up their nostrils.

Pauline The police?

Rufus The louts. I just wish our caring Camden Council would find her a flat.

Alan Bennett They will, only they say if she keeps it like she does the van the other tenants would treat her worse than here.

Rufus Ergo we should be nastier still. Joke. No. Sorry.

Pauline It's funny, though, we heard nothing. And she's outside our house. She's only opposite yours. But then you know us. We're so relaxed. Laid back.

Rufus Yes. You know us. We just do our own thing.

Alan Bennett I see her. You don't.

Pauline and Rufus exit

(*To Alan Bennett 2*) A workmen's truck passes every morning about seven. It always slows down so the driver can bang on her window. Why?

Alan Bennett 2 I'll tell you why. Because people are shits, that's why.

Alan Bennett I wish she'd go.

Alan Bennett 2 Yes. But not yet.

Miss Shepherd enters the desk area

Miss Shepherd Mr Bennett, could you type me out a letter? It's to the College of Cardinals. I was going to phone Mother Teresa but the woman at Directory Enquiries said she drew a blank. "To the College of Cardinals, Rome. Your Eminences. Now it is coming up to the Papal election I would like to suggest that an older and *taller* Pope might be admirable (taller underlined), height counting towards knowledge too, probably. Might I humbly suggest that at the Papal Coronation there could be a not-so-heavy crown, of light plastic possibly, or cardboard, for instance?" I went to Tunbridge Wells yesterday.

Alan Bennett Why Tunbridge Wells?

Miss Shepherd I was told the air was better there. Only I got myself arrested. It was my clothes that did it. I was on the station and the policeman thought I was wearing a nightie. I don't think this style can have got to Tunbridge Wells yet. Mr Bennett, *une autre chose. Je crois que vous étiez en vacances en France.*

Alan Bennett Yes. Er, *oui.*

Miss Shepherd *J'ai étudié en France il y a trente-cinq ans.*

Alan Bennett Really? *Vraiment?*

Alan Bennett 2 You better ask her what. *Qu'est ce qu'elle étudiait?*

Alan Bennett *Qu'est ce que vous étudiez?*

Miss Shepherd *J'étudiais* — What do you want to know for?

Alan Bennett 2 Because it's interesting.

Alan Bennett *Je m'intéresse.*

Miss Shepherd *J'étais à Paris.*

Alan Bennett *Avant la guerre?*

Miss Shepherd What *guerre?*

Alan Bennett *La guerre mondiale numéro deux.*

Miss Shepherd *Oui. La deuxiéme guerre mondiale.*

Alan Bennett *Qu'est ce que vous étudiez?*

Miss Shepherd There you go again. I was studying incognito.

Alan Bennett But what? What were you studying?

Miss Shepherd Music. The pianoforte, possibly. Have you got an old pan scrub? I'm thinking of painting the van. One of those little mop things they use to wash dishes with would do.

Alan Bennett How about a brush?

Miss Shepherd I've got a brush. This is for the first coat.

Alan Bennett 2 She moves slowly round her mobile home thoughtfully touching up the rust patches, looking in her long dress and sun hat much as Vanessa Bell would have looked had she gone in for painting Bedford vans.

Alan Bennett What kind of paint are you using?

Miss Shepherd The shade is crushed mimosa.

Alan Bennett But it's gloss paint. You want car enamel.

Miss Shepherd Don't tell me about paint. I was in the infants' school. I won a prize for painting.

Alan Bennett But it's all lumps. You've got to mix it.

Miss Shepherd I have mixed it, only I went and got some Madeira cake in it.

Miss Shepherd exits

Alan Bennett 2 Cake or no cake, all Miss Shepherd's vehicles ended up looking as if they'd been given a coat of badly made custard or plastered with scrambled egg. Still, there were few occasions on which one saw her genuinely happy and one of these was when she was putting paint on, which she applied as Monet might have done ... and in much the same tones ... standing back to judge the effect of each brush stroke.

Piano music plays in the desk area, Beethoven's Piano Sonata No. 27, Opus 90, in E minor. Alan Bennett listens

Miss Shepherd enters the desk area carrying two plastic sacks

Miss Shepherd Stop the music. Stop it this minute.
Alan Bennett (*switching the music off*) Why? What do you want?
Miss Shepherd You've been away.
Alan Bennett Yes. In Yorkshire.
Miss Shepherd I've been over several times. It's urgent. I want you to write. Asking for special consideration. Because I am disabled. I don't always use a walking stick and that pulls the wool over people's eyes. But what they forget is that I am a bona fide resident of Camden. And there's been no prior notification where legal rights are concerned. I had rheumatic fever as a child. And mumps.
Alan Bennett Miss Shepherd, what is it?
Miss Shepherd What is it? Yellow lines. In the street. They wanted me to shift the van so that they could make the lines continuous and I said I was disabled. Which I am. So now they've put the yellow lines as far as the van and started them the other side.
Alan Bennett So it's still legally parked.
Miss Shepherd For the moment. Only now they've put a removal order under the wiper.
Alan Bennett You could always drive on. Go somewhere else.
Miss Shepherd There may not be enough juice.
Alan Bennett I can get you some up the road.
Miss Shepherd I don't like their petrol. Besides, there may be another problem.
Alan Bennett What problem?
Miss Shepherd Some years ago I saw this recipe for petrol substitute in a church magazine. It was a spoonful of petrol, a gallon of water plus a pinch of something you could buy in every high street. Well, I got it into my head this was bicarbonate of soda. Only I may have remembered it wrong.
Alan Bennett And you put it in the van? Bicarbonate of soda?
Miss Shepherd The recipe may have said sodium nitrate but the man in Boots wouldn't sell me that as it can cause explosions.

Alan Bennett So that's what's in the van now — a spoonful of petrol, a gallon of water and a pinch of bicarbonate of soda?

Miss Shepherd It might go. It might just need a bit of coaxing. In the meantime I want you to write to the council asking for special consideration re parking arrangements. Say you're going to expose it on the BBC. Because I am disabled. People see me walking about perfectly normally but that's because I am making a superhuman effort. Other people who don't make the effort just flop into a wheelchair and their loved ones are foolish enough to push them. What I'm worried about particularly are the wheels. They're under divine protection. If I do get this other vehicle I'd like the wheels transferred.

Alan Bennett Miss Shepherd. What other vehicle? (*To Alan Bennett 2*) Another vehicle!

Miss Shepherd They may be miraculous, the tyres. They've only had to be pumped up once since 1964.

Alan Bennett Miss Shepherd. What "other vehicle"?

Miss Shepherd They only cost me a fiver.

Alan Bennett Miss Shepherd, you said about another vehicle.

Miss Shepherd A van.

Alan Bennett Another van?

Miss Shepherd A titled Catholic lady in the terrace says she may get me one as an act of charity. It's Lady Wiggin only she'd prefer to remain anonymous.

Alan Bennett I bet she would. Will she let you park outside her house?

Miss Shepherd No. She was very specific about that. Meanwhile I thought I'd just give you some of my belongings to keep, just to be on the safe side.

Alan Bennett So where will you go in this new vehicle?

Miss Shepherd I haven't decided. I've got one or two irons in the fire. I may not go anywhere, though Dunstable is one option. I should have the freedom of the land for the pamphlets I've sold on the economy. The least I should have is residents' parking. Of course, even if I did have residents' parking and kept it in the street I'm liable to be attacked again. That would be the worry, possibly. Coming ringing your bell all the time. You never know what's going to happen. What I need is off-street parking.

Alan Bennett So what are you going to do?

Miss Shepherd Play it by ear.

Miss Shepherd exits

Alan Bennett 2 The question now arises: how did she end up in the garden?

Alan Bennett Simple. You invited her.

Alan Bennett 2 Me?

Alan Bennett On what you called "the cork-lined room principle". Her being attacked on the street all the time jeopardized your peace of mind so you couldn't work. That's what you said. I just thought you wanted something to write about.

Alan Bennett 2 I never wanted to write about her. "Oh, another old lady. Right up your street!" Her coming into the garden was a question of will. It was what she wanted all along and you found it easier to say yes than no.

Alan Bennett People could say that was kind.

Alan Bennett 2 Kind is so tame. Come on, help me. Couldn't it be anger? Social conscience? Guilt!

Alan Bennett No.

Alan Bennett 2 Well, whatever it might be let us be plain about one thing: it can't be just being nice. Nice is dull.

Alan Bennett Yes. And anyway I'm not nice.

Rufus and Pauline enter L

Rufus You are a saint.

Pauline An angel.

Rufus Who else would do it?

Pauline Well, we might.

Alan Bennett It's not permanent.

Rufus No, no, no.

Alan Bennett It's only until she decides where she's going to go. Three months at the outside.

Rufus Quite. The open road. The distant highway. I can't see her staying long.

Pauline And it's not as if your garden is much of a feature.

Alan Bennett It's a wild garden.

Pauline Of course it is. Darling. (*She kisses him*) She'll be so grateful.

Pause

Miss Shepherd enters; Rufus and Pauline exit

Miss Shepherd Put it in your garden? I don't know. It might not be convenient.

Alan Bennett No. I've thought it over. Believe me, Miss Shepherd. It's all right.

Miss Shepherd Not convenient for you. Convenient for me. I may have other plans. Besides, the air may not be suitable.

Alan Bennett The air?

Miss Shepherd There's a lot of ivy in your garden. Ivy's poison. I shall have to think about it. You're not doing me a favour, you know. I've got other fish to fry. A man on the pavement told me that if I went south of the river I'd be welcomed with open arms.

Alan Bennett 2 I was to learn that to reject favours when offered was always Miss Shepherd's way. Time had to pass to erase any sense of obligation or gratitude, so that when eventually she did avail herself of the offer and bring the van in the feeling was that she had done me the favour. One laughs, but international diplomacy proceeds along much the same lines. So for a while, the yellow lines still ending at the van and starting the other side, I waited.

A workman enters the garden with a wheelbarrow of manure

Miss Shepherd Mr Bennett. What is the manure doing?

Alan Bennett I got it for the garden.

Miss Shepherd Well, could you move it or put up a notice saying that the smell is the manure. When I bring the van into the garden people may think the smell is me.

Alan Bennett So you've decided to bring it in?

Miss Shepherd I hope I shall have enough room.

Alan Bennett What for?

Miss Shepherd My things. I shall have to put some bags under it, clothes and suchlike, probably. If you don't want all the bags lying about, you could get a tent.

Alan Bennett A tent?

Miss Shepherd It need only be three foot high and by rights it ought to be erected in a meadow, only it would go by the van. Then there are these shatter-proof greenhouses.

Alan Bennett Miss Shepherd. It's only a tiny garden. You're only going to be here for a month or two.

Miss Shepherd Or something could be done with old raincoats, possibly.

Miss Shepherd exits

Alan Bennett 2 Gradually Miss Shepherd evacuates her belongings from the old van until, an empty windowless shell, the council tows it away. And on that same morning, invested by her anonymous donor, Lady Wiggin, with the keys and logbook of her new and as yet unpainted vehicle and once again employing her full repertoire of hand signals, Miss Shepherd drives it into the garden.

Alan Bennett moves into the garden

Miss Shepherd slowly drives the van on L and to its position on the stage, facing UR, at an angle. Having come to a halt, the van begins to roll forward

Alan Bennett Have you put on the handbrake?

Miss Shepherd I am about to do so.

Alan Bennett 2 Whereupon she applies the handbrake with such determination that, like Excalibur, it can never afterwards be released.

Pause

The Lights dim to a night-time setting. Miss Shepherd goes into the back of the van, leaving the doors open

Sometimes when the light is on I get a glimpse of Miss Shepherd praying, and it is seldom a tranquil or a meditative process. The posture of her prayers is more Muslim than Christian. She sits on her haunches, her head bent forward almost touching her knees, the fervour of her intercessions rocking her to and fro. And she prays as combatively as she talks, banging her fist into her hand, mouthing fierce words, God, I feel, as much on the receiving end as I am.

Miss Shepherd The soul in question did *not* witness the incident, though there was hearing of it and seeing of the bodywork. The word accident was mentioned in a local newspaper, allegedly fatal, and a felony committed possibly, but towards the end of Holy Year 1950 I went to Rome on pilgrimage where I was told by an elderly priest of my acquaintance who has since died that a plenary indulgence does cover traffic matters, possibly, though a policeman may not always think it applies, through ignorance possibly.

Lights come up on the van; the light grows, making the van magical and transparent, during the following

O Virgo Fidelis, first leader of all creatures, may evil draw back before thee. I hunger and thirst for the fulfilment of a just era and utterly trust in possible light received, subject always to the Roman Catholic Church in her rights and to amendment.

The Lights fade on the van

Underwood enters as the light fades; we slowly become aware of him. He is a dilapidated figure, tall, thin, trousers well above the ankles, shabby overcoat, Homburg hat and umbrella. For all his slipshod appearance, there is something both genteel and sinister about him. He inspects the van, peering in at the windows

Underwood Lady. (*He taps lightly on the side of the van*) Lady. Are you there, lady? I like the new vehicle. A real spanker. Not a mark on it. Particularly as regards the bodywork. That's clever, Margaret. That's very clever. (*He gives the van a great bang*) Not a fucking scratch. Are you saying your prayers still? How's the piano?

Alan Bennett moves into the garden

Alan Bennett Can I help you?

Underwood Good-evening to you, sir. Finding myself in the vicinity, I am taking this opportunity to pay my compliments to Margaret.

Alan Bennett Margaret?

Underwood I've been out of the game for a while ... you know how it is.

Alan Bennett Miss Shepherd?

Underwood Shepherd, is it?

Alan Bennett (*tapping on the van*) Miss Shepherd!

Underwood Shepherd. Very good.

Alan Bennett She's not there.

Underwood Of course. This isn't *the* van, is it?

Alan Bennett She had another one.

Underwood Very sensible. Very good. Very good. I will bid you good-night then, sir. I will call again when my schedule permits. Good-night, Margaret.

Alan Bennett She's not there.

Underwood goes

Alan Bennett goes back inside

There is a pause

Miss Shepherd appears from the van. She looks after the departing man and raises her stick. She stands there, threatening, with her stick raised

The light fades on Miss Shepherd but she is still visible during the following

Mam enters the desk area

The Light gradually comes back to the desk area, to reveal Mam standing with Alan Bennett watching her

Alan Bennett 2 She'll be wanting to move in next, said my mother.

Mam I got a whiff of her when I came in. It's a right nasty bad dishcloth smell. Well, she's in the garden. Next it'll be the house. What will folk think?

Alan Bennett This is London. Nobody thinks anything.

Mam An educated woman and living like that. Mind you, you're going down the same road.

Alan Bennett Me?

Mam No cloth on the table. No holder for the toilet roll. Given time I could have this place spotless.

Alan Bennett You've got a home. You wouldn't want to live here.

Alan Bennett 2 Yes, she would.

Mam Where does she go to the lav?

Alan Bennett It's something to do with plastic bags.

Mam What sort of plastic bags?

Alan Bennett Stout ones, I hope. Do you want to meet her?

Mam No. With her being educated I shouldn't know what to say. Give us a kiss. When will you be coming up next?

Alan Bennett Soon.

Mam Soon. The thing is, I keep seeing a car in the car park.

Alan Bennett That's slightly to be expected, isn't it?

Mam At night. Watching.

Alan Bennett Are you taking your tablets?

Mam When I remember. She should be in a home. Where does she go to the lav?

Alan Bennett I told you.

Mam Looked after. A place where they'll wash her and make her presentable. I'm surprised they let her roam the streets.

Alan Bennett 2 It's like a fairy story, a parable in which the guilty is gulled into devising a sentence for someone innocent, only to find it is their own doom they have pronounced. Because my mother is much closer to being put in a home than Miss Shepherd.

Mam I do miss your dad. Give us a kiss. I asked our Gordon when he was a pilot did he go behind the clouds?

Alan Bennett And did he?

Mam I forget.

Mam exits

Miss Shepherd moves to the desk area

Miss Shepherd Mr Bennett. I've worked out a way of getting on the wireless. You ask the BBC to give me one of those phone-in programmes, something someone like you could get put on in a jiffy, then I could come into your house and take the calls in the house. Either that or I could get on *Petticoat Line*. I know a darn sight more on moral matters than most of them. I could sing my song over the telephone.

Alan Bennett What song is that?

Miss Shepherd moves to sit down. Alan Bennett manages to slip a newspaper under her as she does so

Miss Shepherd It's a lovely song called *The End of the World*. I won't commit myself to singing it, not at this moment, but I probably would.

Alan Bennett 2 Miss Shepherd is not to know this, but Peter Cook had had a song called *The End of the World*. In 1960 I had thought it silly and fanciful but it had ended up as the finale of *Beyond the Fringe*. Now here it is in life, sung by a creature who makes Peter's wittering park-bench philosophy seem like sober realism. Nor did the similarity end there.

Miss Shepherd Oh, Mr Bennett.

Alan Bennett 2 At one point a toad had found its way into the van and a slug.

Miss Shepherd I think that toad may be in love with the slug. I tried to turn it out and it got very disturbed. I thought at one point it was going to go for me. This phone-in programme, it could all be anonymous. I could be called "The Lady Behind the Curtain". Or "A Woman of Britain". You could take a *nom de plume* view of it. I see the curtain as being here, possibly. Some greeny material would do.

Alan Bennett I thought this was a phone-in.

Miss Shepherd Well?

Alan Bennett It's radio. There's no need for a curtain at all.

Miss Shepherd Yes, well, we can iron out these hiccups when the time comes. I used to listen to *Woman's Hour* only now it's nothing but birth control. I could live behind the curtain and do my broadcasts and the rest of the time be a guest at your television and take in some civilization.

Alan Bennett 2 Live?

Alan Bennett Live?

Miss Shepherd Perhaps there could be gaps in between the talking and they could have quiet classical music. Once upon a time I could have reeled you off some though *Liebestraum* comes to mind. Liszt. I believe he was a Catholic priest.

Alan Bennett Miss Shepherd. Live? Here?

Miss Shepherd *Liebestraum* means Love's Dream, only not the sexy stuff. It's the Love of God and the Sanctification of Labour and so on, which would recommend it to celibates like us, possibly.

Alan Bennett 2 Us? (*He mimes disgust*)

Miss Shepherd Oh, and Mr Bennett, in case I'm attacked again I've got this new alarm system. (*She produces a very faint and squeaky horn and sounds it*)

Alan Bennett I shall never hear that.

Miss Shepherd You will. It's like bats, possibly. Once you've heard it a couple of times your ear will get attuned to it.

Alan Bennett Why is it that both the elderly women in my life want to move in on me?

Alan Bennett 2 They don't like the single life, women. You see, Alan, one of the functions of women is to bring an element of trouble into the otherwise tranquil lives of men. And this is true even of a woman so far fallen from the concerns and competences of the gender as our friend here. Who, frustrated in her ambition to become the Isobel Barnett of her day, now falls back on a political career.

Miss Shepherd Mr Bennett. When I'm elected Prime Minister, would I have to move into Downing Street or could I run things from the van?

Alan Bennett I believe Downing Street is customary.

Miss Shepherd I could park it outside, I suppose. Does Downing Street have parking restrictions?

Alan Bennett I imagine so, but if you're Prime Minister I would think an arrangement could be made.

Miss Shepherd They'd provide me with secretarial help? I couldn't write all the letters myself.

Alan Bennett There are secretaries, I'm sure.

Miss Shepherd I don't want them in the van. I can't be providing room for secretaries. They could crouch outside, I suppose. Or just stand by the window. You do.

Alan Bennett Yes.

Miss Shepherd Mr Bennett.

Alan Bennett Yes?

Miss Shepherd This political party I'm founding. Will you join?

Alan Bennett Is it left or right?

Miss Shepherd It's not left. It's definitely not left. I don't want to let the cat out of the bag too soon about what it stands for in case the other parties pinch the policy.

Alan Bennett What is the policy?

Miss Shepherd I'll tell you so long as you keep it under your hat. Justice.

Alan Bennett Is that it?

Miss Shepherd What more do you want? Everybody wants justice.

Alan Bennett But nothing more specific?

Miss Shepherd Stopping noise is an adamant priority. Fidelis Party, Servants of Justice would jump heavily on drivers making a noise in the evening. Laws re inebriation is another plank of our policy and the able-bodied young called to lessen their occupation with non-mattering things. Plus — and this is crucial — plus the provision of electric chairs.

Alan Bennett Capital punishment?

Miss Shepherd No — well, yes, but what I mean are those electric chair things that some old people have to run about in. I want one.

Alan Bennett Who's going to be in it, the party, what's it called?

Miss Shepherd Fidelis Party, Servants of Justice. Everybody, once they know what it's for.

Alan Bennett But you won't tell them what it's for.

Miss Shepherd I will in due course. It's such a vote-catcher I have to be careful.

Alan Bennett Who are the founder members?

Miss Shepherd You are for one. Then there are one or two elderly nuns I know. There's Mrs Vaughan Williams up the street. There's the man where I buy my batteries, possibly. He's always very civil. And the gentleman who used to come to me for pencils, though I haven't seen him lately. I hope he's not dead. He may just have gone over to biros.

The Lights fade to a night-time setting

Miss Shepherd returns to the van

The Beethoven music played before plays again, though not especially loudly

Suddenly Miss Shepherd erupts from the van

Mr Bennett. Mr Bennett. Stop that. Stop that this minute.

Alan Bennett Stop what?

Miss Shepherd This. The music. I'm a sick woman.

Alan Bennett Why? It's not loud. You can hardly hear it.

Miss Shepherd I don't want to hear it. I don't want to hear it at all.

Alan Bennett Well, tough, because I do.

Miss Shepherd Taking you along, turning you over. No.

Alan Bennett Don't you like music?

Miss Shepherd What's that got to do with anything, what I like? Turn it off.

Alan Bennett I thought the Virgin Mary liked music.

Miss Shepherd Not played at that pitch. Besides, I've got work to do. I'm preparing my manifesto. Mr Bennett, you know you said I wouldn't be able to get nomination papers at the Town Hall.

Alan Bennett I didn't say you wouldn't be able to get them, I said there might be a problem.

Miss Shepherd Mr Bennett.

Alan Bennett Yes?

Miss Shepherd There wasn't a problem. You always say there's going to be a problem and there never is a problem.

Alan Bennett 2 This is true. Miss Shepherd is always mysteriously effective in dealing with officials. Every year she manages to persuade the Post Office to renew her vehicle licence, for instance, though she has no insurance and never submits it for MOT. This success with officials I put down either to her persistence or to their good nature. She puts it down to the intervention of the Holy Ghost. In fact it is none of these. It is the smell. One whiff and anyone with whom she is dealing falls over themselves in order to accommodate her the more speedily to be rid of her and the attendant aroma.

Miss Shepherd Mr Bennett, did you get any more signatures for my nomination?

Alan Bennett I'm afraid I didn't.

Miss Shepherd Well, don't bother. I ran into the Virgin again this afternoon. She was standing outside the Post Office in Parkway. She said three words. Watch and pray.

Alan Bennett You weren't waiting for a bus, were you?

Miss Shepherd What she was meaning is that we should call off the election campaign for Fidelis Party.

Alan Bennett Why?

Miss Shepherd It may be Mrs Thatcher is turning out better than the Virgin expected. She has a low, quiet voice.

Alan Bennett Mrs Thatcher?

Miss Shepherd The Virgin.

Miss Shepherd returns to the van

Alan Bennett 2 Leading from the front, Mrs Thatcher is of course in the van too, and one in my view just as full of garbage as the other. Though the far-fetched notion of a van parked in Downing Street with cabinet ministers meekly queuing at the window for instructions from a wayward and ill-tempered woman would come in the course of the eighties to seem not unrelated to the truth.

The van's lights come on

Underwood enters the garden

Underwood Still here, I see, lady.

The lights of the van instantly go out

What's your name now, Margaret?

Miss Shepherd My name's Mary. Go away.
Underwood Mary is it now? Mary what?

Pause

Mary what? (*He gives a great bang on the side of the van*)
Miss Shepherd I'll call the police.
Underwood You've changed your tune, you two-faced pisshole. Because my understanding was that calling the police is just what you didn't do. Apropos of which I think, madam, another contribution is due. Pay up. (*He gives the van another bang*)

Miss Shepherd starts squeezing her little motor horn. It's a pathetic noise

What the fuck's that?
Miss Shepherd I'm alerting the home-owner.

Alan Bennett comes out

Alan Bennett What's going on? — Good-evening.
Underwood Good-evening to you, sir.
Alan Bennett What's all this din?
Underwood No din, sir. Margaret and I were just taking a stroll down memory lane.
Alan Bennett You came before once.
Underwood I may have done, sir. I may have done. I had probably been attending one of my places of worship.
Miss Shepherd He was banging.
Underwood It's so seldom one gets to the metropolis. One spends one's time making the round of one's acquaintances. Checking which are still, as it were, at their posts. Like Margaret here.
Miss Shepherd Don't Margaret me. That name is buried to sin.
Underwood Friends need to be periodically reminded that one is still extant. Mending fences, as I believe it's called.
Miss Shepherd Not by banging. He was banging.
Underwood A thankless soul. And not over-salubrious. To be quite honest, I don't know how you can stand the Susie Wong.

Underwood raises his hat in farewell and goes

Alan Bennett I thought your name was Mary.
Miss Shepherd It is.
Alan Bennett Why does he call you Margaret?

Miss Shepherd He's taken too much to drink, on an empty stomach, possibly.

Alan Bennett Because I put Mary on the census form. And Shepherd. That's right, isn't it?

Miss Shepherd Yes, yes.

Alan Bennett Mary Shepherd?

Miss Shepherd Subject to the Roman Catholic Church in her rights and to amendment, yes. Mr Bennett. The alarm.

Alan Bennett What about it?

Miss Shepherd You said you wouldn't hear it. You did hear it.

Alan Bennett Yes. (*He heads back inside*)

Miss Shepherd sounds the alarm again

Miss Shepherd Mr Bennett.

Alan Bennett What?

Miss Shepherd There isn't a Susie Wong. It's this manure they keep delivering. That's the Susie Wong.

Alan Bennett Is there anything else you want?

Miss Shepherd No.

Alan Bennett Good-night. (*He goes into the desk area*)

Miss Shepherd sits by the van

Alan Bennett 2 It's obviously not her name. Mary Shepherd is not her name. She's changed it. Not that I blame her. I'd change mine if I could.

Alan Bennett Alan?

Alan Bennett 2 Everything I've written has been an attempt to give some flavour to my name. Alan. It's got as much flavour as a pebble.

Alan Bennett puts some piano music on

Turn it up. Go on. Alan. Go on ...

Alan Bennett is reluctant but does so

Louder.

Alan Bennett 2 raises his hand in expectation of Miss Shepherd appearing

Miss Shepherd moves to the desk area

Miss Shepherd I can hear the music. I can hear it.

Alan Bennett 2 Leave it on.
Miss Shepherd How many more times? I can hear it.

Alan Bennett defers to Miss Shepherd and turns it down, to Alan Bennett 2's disgust

Alan Bennett How can you dislike music? You used to play the piano.
Miss Shepherd How did you know that?
Alan Bennett You told me.
Miss Shepherd I didn't say I didn't like it. I don't want to hear it, that's all.
(*She goes back to the van and suddenly gives a cry that is both inarticulate and heart-rending*)

The cry doesn't seem to affect either Alan Bennett

Alan Bennett 2 Does she speak now? Does she explain?
Alan Bennett She didn't. She didn't ever explain.
Alan Bennett 2 No. But perhaps she should.
Miss Shepherd People are waiting at bus-stops and here is a soul in torment. I was once left alone in a room at the convent ... They didn't leave novices alone normally. I think the other novices had gone to the school to be vaccinated whereas I had been vaccinated already. The room was where we had hymn practice and our milk when it was raining and there was a piano there. I tried it and it was open.

Music — the Beethoven heard before — begins, played on a very poor piano

It wanted tuning and some of the notes were dead but it sounded more beautiful to me than any of the pianos I'd ever played. Then the mistress of the novices must have come in ... crept in possibly, as I never heard her, and suddenly she shut the lid down on my fingers. Said that was what God wanted and I'd been told before. I said, couldn't I just play some hymns for us to sing to? She said that was arguing and I'd never make a nun if I argued.
Alan Bennett Dad used to play hymns on his violin.
Alan Bennett 2 He played the violin. Aunt Eveline played the piano.
Alan Bennett She was a pianist for the silent films.
Alan Bennett 2 For the silent films in Bradford.
Alan Bennett And Uncle George used to sing.
Alan Bennett 2 "Rose of England". "Bless This House".
Alan Bennett In the front room at Grandma's just after the war.

Faintly, growing louder, comes the conclusion of some spectacular piano piece ... Schumann's "Carnaval", say, or the end of Beethoven's Piano

Sonata No 23 in F, Opus 57, The Appassionata. As it ends, Miss Shepherd rises. There is a wave of applause. She sinks into an awkward curtsy as the sound cuts out and she kneels in prayer, her head nearly resting on the floor

The Lights fade

CURTAIN

ACT II

The same

The van is now bright yellow, festooned with odd bits of carpet and with several bulging plastic bags under it

The CURTAIN *rises. The garden and desk area are lit. Alan Bennett and Miss Shepherd are in the garden; Alan Bennett 2 is in the desk area*

Miss Shepherd Is she confined?
Alan Bennett She's in hospital.
Miss Shepherd Under lock and key? No wonder she's depressed.
Alan Bennett She wanders the streets.
Miss Shepherd Everybody likes a bit of fresh air.
Alan Bennett At four o'clock in the morning? She needed treatment.
Miss Shepherd Are you next of kin?
Alan Bennett Yes.
Miss Shepherd They're the ones you've got to watch — the next of kin. They can't touch you, legally. A year and a day. If you keep out of their clutches for a year and a day you're free. That's the law.
Alan Bennett Miss Shepherd. She's not insane. She's depressed.
Miss Shepherd With you trying to put her away I'm not surprised.

Miss Shepherd exits

Alan Bennett 2 So I get rid of one old lady and take in the other. These days it's almost as if we're married. "How's your old lady?" people say.
Alan Bennett "Still there."
Alan Bennett 2 "Your mother died, didn't she?"
Alan Bennett "No. She was in hospital, only now she's in a home. Still, she doesn't know where she is, so that's a blessing."
Alan Bennett 2 "And where is she?"
Alan Bennett "Weston-super-Mare."
Alan Bennett 2 Except you're seldom so frank as that. When people ask you don't say she's in a home; you lie and say she's with my brother in Bristol.
Alan Bennett Putting her in a home seems some sort of failure.
Alan Bennett 2 And giving this one a home?
Alan Bennett That seems a failure too.
Alan Bennett 2 Actually that's quite neat. I like that.

Alan Bennett (*amiably*) Oh, piss off.

There is a distant sound of a car approaching, getting nearer all the time

Suddenly (and possibly with a bang) Miss Shepherd erupts on to the stage in a three-wheeler Robin Reliant. Her hand signals still immaculate, she comes to a halt and gets out. She wears the car key round her neck

(*To Miss Shepherd*) Where will you park it?
Miss Shepherd In the residents' parking.
Alan Bennett You haven't got a permit.
Miss Shepherd I have. I got one yesterday.
Alan Bennett You never told me.
Miss Shepherd You'd only have raised objections if I had.
Alan Bennett Have you insured it?
Miss Shepherd I don't need insuring. It's like the van. I'm insured in heaven.
Alan Bennett So who pays if you have an accident? The Pope?
Miss Shepherd I shan't have an accident.
Alan Bennett What if you run into something?
Miss Shepherd I shan't run into anything. I'm an experienced driver. I drove ambulances in the black-out.
Alan Bennett What if someone runs into you?

Pause

Miss Shepherd. What if someone runs into you?
Miss Shepherd (*fiercely*) You've no business saying that.

Pause

Why do you say that? No-one is going to run into me. No-one. (*She gets into her car*)

Pause

Where's the key?
Alan Bennett What key?
Miss Shepherd The car key. I put it down.
Alan Bennett I haven't got it.

Miss Shepherd gets out of the car again

Miss Shepherd You have. You've taken it.
Alan Bennett I have not.

Miss Shepherd (*shouting*) You're lying. You don't want me to have the car so you've taken the key.

Alan Bennett Don't shout.

Miss Shepherd I have to shout because of your ignorance. The gate going bang bang all hours of the day and night, I'd be better off in a ditch. Give me the key.

Alan Bennett I haven't got your sodding key. What's that round your neck? This. This.

Alan Bennett pushes Miss Shepherd and she falls against the car

The key. The fucking key. Shouldn't you say sorry?

Miss Shepherd (*getting back into the car*) I've no time for sorry. Sorry is for God.

Miss Shepherd reverses the car off

Alan Bennett 2 That was the first and practically the only time I ever touched her. It wasn't her calling me a liar that made me, even in this scarcely injurious way, suddenly violent. It was that she was mad. I knew I had never had the key and her need to convince me that I had was like someone suffering from delusions who needs to convince you of their truth. It was my mother.

Alan Bennett (*to Alan Bennett 2*) It's always Mam you compare her with. They're not the same. I don't like them even sharing the same sentence.

Alan Bennett 2 Miss Shepherd is painting her new vehicle with what seems not so much a brush as a hard stick and looking in her peaked cap like one of those disconsolate German generals surrendering at Stalingrad.

Miss Shepherd enters the garden

Miss Shepherd Mr Bennett. I don't like the three-wheeler standing in the street. If you pushed the van in front of your window I could get the Reliant in there beside it. There's tons of room.

Alan Bennett You mean I have the van *and* the Reliant?

Miss Shepherd It would mean easier access for the Reliant from a coming and going aspect.

Alan Bennett Not easier access for me. I can only just get to my own door as it is.

Miss Shepherd I've had guidance that's where the Reliant should go, in terms of vandals, possibly.

Alan Bennett Guidance from whom?

Miss Shepherd I'm not at liberty to speak. I think I may contact my social worker.

Alan Bennett What for? You always say you don't want the social worker.
Miss Shepherd (*getting back in the van*) I've had guidance she might help.

The Lights change

The Social Worker enters

Social Worker Perhaps we should try and look at the situation in terms of Miss Shepherd's needs.
Alan Bennett I prefer to call them wants.
Social Worker She needs somewhere to live.
Alan Bennett She's got somewhere to live. The van. She wants somewhere besides.
Miss Shepherd (*from the van*) There is room. Lashings of room. As a garden it's a disgrace.
Alan Bennett I don't want a used-car lot.
Miss Shepherd He keeps getting all this manure but it never comes to anything.
Alan Bennett The van's in front of my door. I don't want the car in front of my window.
Miss Shepherd Weeds, that's all it is. Some of them poisonous. I'd be doing him a service. A nice little yellow three-wheeler instead of loads of useless ivy.
Alan Bennett No.
Miss Shepherd It's like I said. He'll always put scruples in the way. Through having been a communist possibly. (*She closes her window*)

Miss Shepherd exits from the van

Alan Bennett She only wants the car to put her clothes in. It's just a second home.
Social Worker Do you have a second home?
Alan Bennett Yes. But not cheek by jowl with my first.
Social Worker Everybody likes to get out. You see, I've talked to Mary ——
Alan Bennett Mary who?
Social Worker Mary, your Lady in the Van. Didn't you know her name was Mary?
Alan Bennett I suppose I did. I always call her Miss Shepherd.
Social Worker We all have names. Perhaps if you called her by her name and she called you by yours?
Alan Bennett What's that?
Social Worker Alan.
Alan Bennett Oh yes, that.

Social Worker Alan, Mary. You never know, it might be easier to talk things through.

Alan Bennett Through? There is no through. How do you talk things through with someone who has conversations with the Virgin Mary? You talk things through with Isaiah Berlin, maybe, who in comparison with Miss Shepherd is a man of few words, but you do not talk things through with her because you don't get through.

Social Worker Alan. I'm getting a bit of hostility here. I realize that for you this may be a steep learning curve —

Alan Bennett No. It is not a steep learning curve. I have never been on a so-called learning curve. I am as likely to be found on a learning curve as I am on the ski slopes at Zermatt. And besides, her name isn't Mary.

Social Worker Oh? Why?

Alan Bennett I don't know. Some people seem to think it's Margaret. And that it isn't even Shepherd.

Social Worker I have her down as Mary.

Alan Bennett Yes, and you presumably have her down as a rational human being.

The Lights change

The Social Worker exits

There comes the sound of Miss Shepherd revving the Reliant off stage

Alan Bennett 2 The Reliant being, as the social worker points out, Miss Shepherd's second home, what more natural than that Miss Shepherd should spend her weekends there? And so at 7.30 this Sunday morning her slippered foot toys with the accelerator, bringing a breath of Brands Hatch to the Sunday morning street and otherwise decent liberals curse her under their breath as they stagger from their beds to retrieve the papers from the doormat.

The revving slows down and stops

Putting some rubbish out, I see what I take to be a snail or slug clinging to the side of the bin. It is a small brown turd with one hair clinging to it, presumably an escapee from one of Miss Shepherd's plastic bags.

There comes the sound of Miss Shepherd trying to start the car and not managing it

Miss Shepherd enters carrying a car battery

Miss Shepherd Mr Bennett ... Mr Bennett. My battery seems to be flat. I'll pay for the electricity. I'll pay for your time.
Alan Bennett I don't want paying for my time.
Alan Bennett 2 What I want paying for is the pitying smiles of passers-by when they see me fiddling under the bonnet of such a motorized joke.

Alan Bennett carries the battery inside

Miss Shepherd Make sure it's good electricity. I think the electricity in the afternoon is better quality than that in the evening, possibly. It used to be better, just after the war. These days they dilute it.
Alan Bennett 2 The wing of the car, I see today, is made of papier mâché. Someone has put their fist through it, Miss Shepherd's repair job consisting of stuffing the hole with Kleenex, which she trims with a pair of nail scissors before giving it a coat of crushed mimosa.

Alan Bennett carries the battery out and off stage to the car during the following

Miss Shepherd When you put it back, see you screw the nuts tight.
Alan Bennett No need for that. Only connect, that's all that's required.
Alan Bennett 2 Though catch E. M. Forster taking time off from writing *Howards End* in order to fit an Exide battery into a clapped-out three-wheeler.

Alan Bennett returns

Miss Shepherd Mr Bennett. I may go away any time. Brighton possibly. Or St Albans. I need the air. So don't worry if you don't see me. Or I may go on retreat in Cornwall with some nuns I know. I've got one or two irons in the fire. Though, Mr Bennett ——
Alan Bennett Yes?
Miss Shepherd I'm not committing myself. I may not go at all.

Miss Shepherd exits

Alan Bennett 2 In her mind, Miss Shepherd was a frequent traveller, a figure of unexplained absences and abrupt departures. She was always threatening to go away but seldom did. This time, though, it seemed she had.

The Lights change. The van is dark and silent

Alan Bennett collects his bicycle from off stage and wheels it into the garden. He looks at the van

Alan Bennett Miss Shepherd? Miss Shepherd?

Rufus and Pauline enter the garden

Rufus What's happened to Stirling Moss? I haven't seen her at the wheel recently.

Alan Bennett Taking a well-earned break, I imagine. The Dordogne possibly.

Pauline Really?

Rufus Pauline.

Pauline Oh, sorry. Only it's one of the places we'd thought of moving to.

Rufus Yes, though that includes most localities this side of the Arctic Circle. I take it she's been in a mental hospital?

Alan Bennett Why?

Rufus She asked me the other day if I had the Pope's private address. I said I thought Rome would probably get him.

Alan Bennett Was that recently?

Rufus Three or four weeks ago.

Alan Bennett It's just that I haven't seen her around for a bit.

Rufus I'm right in thinking that large many-contoured stain on the back of her frock denotes incontinence?

Alan Bennett Well, I don't think it's a fashion statement.

Pauline Oh, darling. What you must be hoping is that one of these days she'll just slip away.

Rufus Don't you believe it. That's what happens in plays. In life going downhill is an uphill job.

Pauline How's your mother?

Alan Bennett Same. Sits. Smiles. Sleeps.

Pauline nods caringly

Pauline Are you all right?

Alan Bennett Me? Yes, why?

Pauline Not upset about your play?

Alan Bennett No.

Pauline I saw a good review the other day.

Alan Bennett I was told they were all good.

Pauline Oh, they are, I'm sure.

Rufus We enjoyed it. I'm amazed how you remember it all.

Pauline The one I saw was particularly perceptive about you.

Alan Bennett Really? Saying what?

Pauline That you couldn't make your mind up.

Alan Bennett What about?

Pauline Anything really. It meant in a good way.

Alan Bennett stares at the van

Are you on tonight?

Alan Bennett Yes. I'm just going down there now. (*He heads away, but stops and knocks tentatively on the side of the van*)

Pauline and Rufus exit

Alan Bennett 2 Can I put an idea into your head?

Alan Bennett No. I'm going down to the theatre.

Alan Bennett 2 I think she's either dying or dead.

Alan Bennett No. She's away. (*He taps on the window*) Miss Shepherd. Miss Shepherd.

Alan Bennett 2 "Did you know she was dead?" the coroner will ask. "Was there no smell?" "Oh, there was always a smell."

Alan Bennett I'm thinking of Mam, who is neither dead nor alive. Dying is better.

Alan Bennett 2 Yes. So look in.

Alan Bennett No.

Alan Bennett 2 Are you scared?

Alan Bennett No.

Alan Bennett 2 Not of the body. You're scared this may be the end of the story and now I'm going to have to tell it.

Alan Bennett I'm scared, maybe, but you're pleased.

Alan Bennett 2 No. I'm fascinated.

Alan Bennett You're contemptible.

Alan Bennett cycles off

Alan Bennett 2 I think of her at the wheel of her khaki ambulance; dodging the craters and the heaps of rubble; seeing the dusty dead brought out and kneeling sometimes in packed churches; sitting around in the canteen waiting for the siren to go. Love once, even, maybe. The time of her life.

There come distant sirens and the sound of the Blitz, which fade leaving a faint light which grows. The van begins to glow with light, even splits in two perhaps, forming a kind of diptych with Miss Shepherd illuminated by a shaft of light

Miss Shepherd No, there was never love. But the soul in question, frustrated in her vocation through want of seeing by the sisters, has loved thee and striven to serve thee as a nun on her own, as it were, solo, living under a rule, with diet restricted, her cell this van, sustained only by supplementary benefit and the sale of the occasional pencil. (*The prayer becomes an argument, with her banging her fist etc.*) If sin there was it was by omission only, as on the day in question the lady-seller was stationary in her vehicle and scrupulous as thy servant has always been in the employment of hand signals and the correct use of the mirror, nevertheless the young man in question, through having had too much to drink, on an empty stomach, possibly, contrives to collide with the van. As was claimed, fatally. The lady-seller was blameless, though she did make her confession later — in France, it was, and even if the priest was well stricken in years and deaf, he did understand English, possibly. And even if he didn't, being a consecrated priest the words of his mouth alone would suffice to absolve me, the lady-seller, of this offence of which in any case she is innocent not only by the laws of God but also by the Highway Code. So, O Blessed Mother, untaint me of all sin so that I may stand before thee undefiled — Lord have mercy, Christ have mercy ...... (*The prayer turns into a mutter, possibly in Latin*)

The Lights fade inside and out of the van; the van closes up

Alan Bennett arrives back from the theatre on his bike. He stops and listens to the now dark van

Alan Bennett 2 comes up behind him and puts his hand on his shoulder

Alan Bennett Should I look now, do you think?

Alan Bennett 2 It'll wait. Besides, it's too dark. Tomorrow would be better. Perhaps then you should take some photographs.

Alan Bennett Of the van? She never liked that.

Alan Bennett 2 Of the van ... and if she's taken away, all that. As a personal record?

Alan Bennett There were so many things I should have asked her.

Alan Bennett 2 She wouldn't have answered. Still, now she's gone you can make it up. Invent. You see, Alan ——

Alan Bennett Yes, Alan?

Alan Bennett 2 You must learn to lie a little. Not long dead is Bruce Chatwin. (*To Alan Bennett*) Now he could lie.

Alan Bennett Yes. But Bruce Chatwin worked for Sotheby's.

Alan Bennett 2 People like it when you lie.

Alan Bennett Do you want to go to bed?

Alan Bennett 2 Why not? You know this is only a metaphor.

Alan Bennett That's what they all say.

The Lights change. It is morning. The van is closed and dark

Alan Bennett approaches the van followed by Alan Bennett 2

Miss Shepherd.
Alan Bennett 2 It is over. She is dead.

Pause

Alan Bennett Miss Shepherd.
Alan Bennett 2 Go on. Open the door.
Alan Bennett Hold on.
Alan Bennett 2 She's either dead or she's in a coma. (*He pushes Alan Bennett*)
Alan Bennett Give over. This could be really sad.
Alan Bennett 2 I know. I can't wait.

Alan Bennett very nervously opens the back door of the van, face screwed up in disgust and anticipation, with Alan Bennett 2 peering over his shoulder

Miss Shepherd materializes on the other side of the stage in a wheelchair and bears down on them at full speed

Miss Shepherd What are you doing?

Alan Bennett 2 leaps back, startled

Alan Bennett 2 Fuck!
Miss Shepherd Looking at my things.
Alan Bennett I thought you were ill.
Alan Bennett 2 (*prompting him*) Dead.
Alan Bennett Dead.
Miss Shepherd Dead? Me?
Alan Bennett 2 You were concerned.
Alan Bennett I was concerned.
Miss Shepherd You were nosy.
Alan Bennett I hadn't seen you.
Miss Shepherd Of course you hadn't seen me. I told you I was on retreat. I'm not dead. You'll know when I'm dead.
Alan Bennett I'm sorry. (*Then, rounding on Alan Bennett 2*) Though you're not, are you?
Alan Bennett 2 I didn't know it was just a retreat. I thought she'd abandoned the struggle altogether.

Miss Shepherd Me! Dead!

Alan Bennett 2 Anyway, think of it as a dry run. After all, one day it'll happen.

Miss Shepherd I shan't die in a hurry, I can tell you.

The Lights change

Alan Bennett 2 And she didn't. So for the time being, years even, we went on much as before. There were occasional rows, like the saga of the eiderdown she wanted put on the van roof.

Alan Bennett Miss Shepherd, it'll get all soggy.

Miss Shepherd Not soggy. Weather-beaten.

Alan Bennett 2 And there was always the banging of the gate. One of her remedies, some chewing gum she wanted sticking on the latch to deaden the noise.

Alan Bennett Chewing gum?

Miss Shepherd It doesn't matter which flavour.

Alan Bennett 2 But now it is evening, say, and warm. With a fan made from a cornflakes packet, Miss Shepherd is taking the air.

Miss Shepherd produces her cornflake-packet fan from the chair. Alan Bennett 2 takes hold of the wheelchair, puts Alan Bennett behind it and indicates he push it c

Miss Shepherd How's your mother?

Alan Bennett The same. Doesn't remember me now.

Miss Shepherd I'm not surprised. She doesn't see you very often. Will you write about me?

Alan Bennett looks enquiringly at Alan Bennett 2

Alan Bennett I don't know. She never said this.

Alan Bennett 2 So?

Miss Shepherd You write about your mother.

Alan Bennett She didn't say that either.

Alan Bennett 2 No, but why shouldn't she?

Miss Shepherd You write about her all the time, one way and another. You use your mother.

Alan Bennett (*looking at Alan Bennett 2*) That's what writers do.

Miss Shepherd Me next, I suppose.

Alan Bennett Y — possibly.

Miss Shepherd Does she know you write about her?

Alan Bennett How can she? She doesn't know who she is.

Miss Shepherd I prefer that.

Alan Bennett What?

Miss Shepherd The incognito position.
Alan Bennett Mum's the word.
Miss Shepherd Yes. Mum is always the word. I'm all for mum. Mr Bennett. Push me up there a bit.

Alan Bennett pushes her US

Let go.

He does so and the chair rolls slowly downstage with Miss Shepherd smiling slightly

Miss Shepherd Mr Bennett.
Alan Bennett What?
Miss Shepherd Will you do it again?
Alan Bennett (*to Alan Bennett 2*) It's supposed to be half-past eleven at night.
Alan Bennett 2 So what? It makes a nice ending to the scene. (*He pushes her up again and lets go*)

She rolls slowly down, smiling and obviously enjoying herself. Alan Bennett and Alan Bennett 2 are smiling too

Alan Bennett 2 pushes Miss Shepherd off stage

The Lights change

Alan Bennett 2 returns. A Doctor enters the desk area

Doctor As you can appreciate, it's difficult to take a history but I'm right in thinking she hasn't been a smoker?
Alan Bennett No.
Doctor Not been a smoker, doesn't drink, all things considered a very healthy woman.
Alan Bennett You think?
Doctor She's beginning to be incontinent, of course, but she has a good appetite and could, I imagine ... and in the right circumstances ... go on for years. The question is, are these the right circumstances?

There is an awkward silence

Let me put it another way. This is a woman who has broken her hip and developed pneumonia. At this age it is what one expects. And of course in someone younger and in better circumstances we would give them antibiotics. At your mother's age and in her state of mind, one wonders if this is altogether kind.

Alan Bennett If you don't give her antibiotics what will happen?
Doctor She may recover or not. She could just sleep away.
Alan Bennett Is it my decision?
Doctor Is there anyone else?
Alan Bennett Can we not wait and see if she improves?
Doctor Certainly. With or without the antibiotics?

Alan Bennett says nothing

No. Well, we'll play it by ear. You mustn't reproach yourself. You've done all — more than could be expected.

Miss Shepherd comes on slowly in her chair, L

The Doctor exits

Alan Bennett moves to Miss Shepherd in the garden

Miss Shepherd Mr Bennett. Where've you been? I've rung the bell twice.
Alan Bennett Seeing my mother.
Miss Shepherd How is she?
Alan Bennett She's very poorly.
Miss Shepherd Yes? Well, I've not been well again myself.
Alan Bennett She's in a coma.
Miss Shepherd Probably just having forty winks.
Alan Bennett Miss Shepherd. She is dying.
Miss Shepherd Can't be doing with company, probably. She should be grateful she doesn't have to cope with letters from Mr Campbell Adamson.
Alan Bennett The Chairman of the CBI?
Miss Shepherd He's wanting to change the Abbey National from being a building society into a bank and he needs my consent. I have voting rights, apparently.
Alan Bennett Do you have something in the Abbey National then?
Miss Shepherd If a person had put money on deposit in one name and that was the name the vote was in, but that wasn't their real name, would that be against the law?
Alan Bennett Why, did you do that?
Miss Shepherd (*banging her hand*) I did not say that. If a soul did. A creature. Not me. It is not me.
Alan Bennett What other name?
Miss Shepherd How many more times? I am in an incognito position. Take an anonymous view of it. Anyway, now you're here I want some shopping done.

Alan Bennett You ought to go yourself. You should try and walk more.
Miss Shepherd I do walk.
Alan Bennett I never see you.
Miss Shepherd That's because you're not about in the middle of the night. I want some batteries and some sherbet lemons.
Alan Bennett I got you sherbet lemons last time.
Miss Shepherd You never know when you'll run out. I'm on them again now. I don't want to have to go off them.
Alan Bennett Is there anything else?
Miss Shepherd No.
Alan Bennett Do you want some towels?
Miss Shepherd Towels? What do I want towels for?
Alan Bennett 2 I did not mean towels. I meant the kind of towels my mother used to send me next door to the draper's and babies' knitwear shop for when I was a boy; towels that came in plain brown-paper parcels; towels that could not be mentioned. And the reason why I am mentioning them is because I can see one such towel (probably an incontinence pad) drying by the electric ring inside the van. The stench is staggering.
Miss Shepherd Can you smell a smell?
Alan Bennett I can, yes.
Miss Shepherd It isn't me. It's that Greek restaurant. They do things on sticks.
Alan Bennett You're not planning on going back to bed? I don't think you should. The longer you stay in bed the weaker you get. You were in bed all last week.
Miss Shepherd I was not in bed. I might appear to be lying down with the blankets over me and my eyes may be closed and at a casual glance ill-disposed persons might think it was bed. But they are wrong. I can't afford to be in bed with my schedule. I've got a hundred and one things to do.
Alan Bennett What I'm trying to say ——
Miss Shepherd You put your mother in a home, that's what you're trying to say. And now it's my turn. You want me taken away again.
Alan Bennett Again? How do you mean, again?

Miss Shepherd won't answer. She shakes her head and gets into the van

Would you like me to make you a cup of coffee?
Miss Shepherd No. I don't want you to go to all that trouble. I'll just have half a cup.

Alan Bennett sees something on the path. He goes off and returns, puts on kitchen gloves then over the gloves two plastic shopping bags, picks whatever it is up and puts it in the bin

Rufus and Pauline enter

Alan Bennett Sorry — there's something wrong with her face as well. Her face is all swollen but she won't see a doctor.

Rufus Wise woman. Look at it from her point of view. Doctor calls, he takes one look.

Pauline Or she.

Rufus Say again, my love?

Pauline The doctor. He or she.

Rufus (*controlling himself with an effort*) Doctor, gender unspecified, takes one look at the ailing derelict and promptly despatches her to whatever hospital/stroke bin can be browbeaten into accommodating her. Result: dead inside six months. Winkle her out of her vehicles and she will snuff it, no question. Which is what you want, of course! Ah, Uncle, I see the plan. Then quite agree. Urge doctor on her by all means.

Alan Bennett Actually her face isn't exactly swollen. It's as if there are little sacs of fluid attached to her cheek. I suppose what they really look like are used contraceptives.

There is a shocked silence

Rufus Now I've seen it all. Forget Mother Teresa. This is our neighbour who thinks nothing of going out in rubber gloves to retrieve the discarded faeces of an evil-smelling old bat who now has used condoms dangling from her cheeks. Pauline, my dear, this is goodness.

Alan Bennett (*apologetically*) Actually they're not as long as condoms; that's just what they remind me of.

The Lights cross-fade to the desk area

Rufus and Pauline exit; a Social Worker enters the desk area

Social Worker I've talked to Mary.

Alan Bennett Or Margaret.

Social Worker Or Margaret. Miss Shepherd anyway. She isn't too well and you're right to be concerned about her, though we ought, I think, to look at her all-round well-being. (*She smiles*)

Alan Bennett says nothing

She tells me you don't encourage her to get out and lead a more purposeful life and put obstacles in her way.

Alan Bennett I don't encourage her to think she can become Prime Minister;
I do encourage her to try and get to the supermarket.
Social Worker These days women have other needs. They can do both.
Alan Bennett Become Prime Minister?
Social Worker No. They can pursue a career or whatever. Homemaking is
not the only option. Because her chosen lifestyle is less conventional than
yours ... we must try not to be too judgmental. You see, a carer will often
feel that he or she has the right to dictate ——
Alan Bennett Excuse me. May I stop you? Do not call me the carer. I am
not the carer. I hate caring. I hate the thought. I hate the word. I do not care
and I do not care for. I am here; she is there. There is no caring.
Social Worker It's interesting that she irritates you and yet she stays. When
you are saying she should be in hospital, is it really a way of saying
something you can't admit: namely that you want to be rid of her?
Unmarried daughters, single sons ... they often have this problem ——
Alan Bennett She is not my mother.
Social Worker — and it isn't one a doctor can always solve.
Alan Bennett I don't particularly want to be rid of her.
Social Worker Why? It would be entirely natural if you did.
Alan Bennett You're saying that the problem is I want her to go, and when
I say I don't want her to go you say that's a problem too. Is this what's called
counselling?
Social Worker Alan, I'm sensing that hostility again.

Pause

You see, I am wondering whether, having cared for Mary as it were single-
handed all these years, you don't, understandably, resent it when the
professionals lend a hand.
Alan Bennett No. Though I resent it when the professionals, as you call it,
turn up every three months or so and try to tell me what this woman, whom
I have coped with on a daily basis for fifteen years, is like.
Social Worker What is she like?
Alan Bennett Mary, as you call her, is a bigoted, blinkered, cantankerous,
devious, unforgiving, self-centred, rank, rude, car-mad cow. Which, Miss
Aileen McNiff Naff, is to say nothing of her flying faeces and her ability
to extrude from her withered buttocks turds of such force that they land a
yard from the back of the van and their presumed point of exit.
Alan Bennett 2 Though of course you didn't say a word of that.
Alan Bennett No.
Alan Bennett 2 People would think that was because you were too nice. It's
actually because you're too timid.

Alan Bennett Yes. Only this being England, timid is good too.
Social Worker I think this has been very helpful. I'll see about getting a
  doctor.

The Lights come up on the garden

  The Doctor enters

Doctor I gather she's lived in the van for some time.
Alan Bennett Yes.
Doctor Don't you mind that?
Alan Bennett Me? Sometimes.
Doctor And how old now?
Alan Bennett Seventy-eight.

Pause. Alan Bennett, the Doctor and the Social Worker go up to the van

  Hallo. Hallo. Miss Shepherd. The doctor has come.
Miss Shepherd (*from the van*) Is it a man doctor?
Alan Bennett Yes.
Miss Shepherd I don't want a man doctor. Don't they have a woman?
Doctor I only want to take your pulse.
Miss Shepherd Which hand? Do you have a preference?
Doctor No.

Miss Shepherd puts her hand through the window

Miss Shepherd It's normally cleaner than that.

*The Doctor takes Miss Shepherd's pulse and peers in to try and look at her
face*

  Have you finished with this hand?
Doctor Miss Shepherd. I'd like to take you into hospital for a day or so, just
  to run some tests.
Miss Shepherd I've always had great faith in onions.
Doctor Yes. Onions can only take you so far, medically speaking.
Alan Bennett She won't go to hospital.
Social Worker How do you know?
Alan Bennett Ask her.

The Social Worker is about to do so but turns to Alan Bennett

Social Worker Would she go to the day centre? She could be looked at there.
Alan Bennett She won't go to the day centre.

Social Worker Are you sure? Have you asked her?
Alan Bennett I *know.*

The Social Worker has a brief word with Miss Shepherd and comes back

Social Worker She'll go.

The Doctor and the Social Worker leave

Miss Shepherd Mr Bennett. The social worker was wanting to know my next of kin. I don't want my next of kin broadcast so I said I didn't have any. Only I've left an envelope in the van. But keep that under your hat. Mr Bennett. They won't keep me in?
Alan Bennett No. They're going to give you a bath and put you in clean clothes and do some tests.
Miss Shepherd Will they leave me to it?
Alan Bennett Where?
Miss Shepherd In the bath. I can bath myself. I won awards for that.
Alan Bennett Yes. I remember.
Miss Shepherd Mr Bennett.
Alan Bennett Yes?
Miss Shepherd It won't look as if I'm being taken away?
Alan Bennett Taken away where?
Miss Shepherd Where they take people because they're not right, possibly. Do they do that still?
Alan Bennett Sometimes, though you need a lot of signatures.
Miss Shepherd They pretend things to get you there sometimes. That's the danger with next of kin. It's one of their tricks. They might just be pretending it's a day centre.
Alan Bennett No.
Miss Shepherd I was had like that once before.
Alan Bennett 2 She kept on about next of kin. Did you not wonder about it?
Alan Bennett I used to wonder if she died whether the next of kin would all come crawling out of the woodwork.
Alan Bennett 2 Well, let's see. Perhaps they should.

An Ambulance Man enters the garden with a van with a hoist, plus the Social Worker

Ambulance Man Miss Shepherd.

During the following, the Ambulance Man lifts Miss Shepherd out of her van and into her wheelchair

Miss Shepherd I'm a bit behindhand with things so there may be a bit of a Susie Wong.

Ambulance Man Put your arm round my neck.

Miss Shepherd Oh. I've never gone in for this kind of thing much.

Alan Bennett 2 I note how with none of my own distaste the ambulance driver does not hesitate to touch her and put his arm round her as he lowers her into the chair. I note too his careful rearrangement of her greasy clothing, pulling the skirt down over her knees in the interest of modesty.

Miss Shepherd I'm coming back, you know. It's not a toe in the water job.

Social Worker Is there anything you want to take and have us wash?

Miss Shepherd Why? Most of my things are clean. Mr Bennett. Keep an eye on the van. It's got all my papers in it. And if I don't like it, I can come back?

Social Worker Of course.

Ambulance Man I'll just take you to the ambulance.

The Ambulance Man wheels Miss Shepherd on to the lift at the back of his van

Miss Shepherd I was an ambulance driver myself once. During the war. I knew Kensington in the black-out.

The lift ascends with the wheelchair on it

Alan Bennett 2 The chair goes up on the lift and in this small ascension when she slowly rises above the level of the garden wall there is a vagabond nobility about her, a derelict Nobel Prize-winner she looks, her grimy face set in a kind of resigned satisfaction.

Miss Shepherd Could we do that again? I'd like another go.

Ambulance Man When you come back.

The Ambulance Man settles Miss Shepherd in the van and they drive off

Social Worker I don't think she will come back.

Alan Bennett No?

Social Worker She's quite frail.

Alan Bennett Can you visit?

Social Worker Why?

Alan Bennett I thought I could take her some flowers. That is, if she decides to stay. Nobody can ever have given her flowers in her life.

Social Worker She won't stay at the day centre, of course. Once she's been assessed she'll go on somewhere else. A council home, possibly, or a hospital.

Alan Bennett Will she not have a choice?

Social Worker In theory, but people are generally quite sensible.

The Social Worker exits

Alan Bennett 2 What are the flowers about? Guilt?
Alan Bennett Maybe.
Alan Bennett 2 I don't see why. She's been a cow.
Alan Bennett (*laughing*) Yes.
Alan Bennett 2 Has she, in all these years, ever said thank you?
Alan Bennett No. Which is a kind of triumph, really. I wouldn't want her
to break her duck now. But I don't want to lose touch.
Alan Bennett 2 Oh no. Nor do I. I want to follow her to the finish, wherever
that might be.
Alan Bennett That wouldn't be guilt?
Alan Bennett 2 God, no. That, one must hope, might be art.

Alan Bennett exits, leaving Alan Bennett 2

The Lights fade to a night-time setting; the van seems empty and isolated

*Alan Bennett returns with some flowers and is about to go into the house
when there is the squeaking of Miss Shepherd's alarm horn, but so faintly
he is not certain he's heard it*

Alan Bennett Miss Shepherd?

The van door opens and Miss Shepherd sits up inside

Miss Shepherd I'm a bit done up. I came back under my own steam.
Alan Bennett Came back? What for?
Miss Shepherd I wasn't stopping in that place. A woman said my face rang
a bell, was I ever in Holloway? And wouldn't give over. They gave me
some mince. She said, "You'll find the mince here is a step up from the
mince in Holloway." I don't know about the mince in Holloway, or
anywhere else.
Alan Bennett You look nice and clean.
Miss Shepherd That will be the bath. They let me do it myself, only the nurse
came and gave me some finishing touches. She said I'd come up a treat. The
soap they use comes in a bottle. I might invest in some of it myself. I mean,
what would I be doing in Holloway?
Alan Bennett 2 Give her the flowers.
Alan Bennett I nearly forgot. I bought you these.
Miss Shepherd Flowers? What do I want with flowers? They only die. I've
enough on my plate without flowers.
Alan Bennett (*to Alan Bennett 2*) Thanks very much. (*To Miss Shepherd*)
You won't often have been given flowers.

Miss Shepherd Who says? I've had bigger flowers than these and with ribbons on. They don't compare.

Alan Bennett I can give you something to put them in.

Miss Shepherd I've got a Horlicks jar they'll go in. There's some old Horlicks in it still but it won't do them any harm. Here. If you want water there's generally some collects in the dustbin lid.

Miss Shepherd hands Alan Bennett a jar; he puts the flowers in it

Not been given flowers. There were always flowers. Flowers were routine. And I'd smile and curtsy. There was a piano at the day centre. (*She says this as if she has just been talking about the piano, as in a way she has*) I didn't try and play it. I don't know that my fingers will run to it now. They had the wireless on all the time. Music. How are people supposed to avoid it?

Alan Bennett Do you want to avoid it?

Miss Shepherd (*vehemently*) The soul in question was instructed to avoid it. Directions were given, sacrifices made, possibly. It was my mother I got it from. She was keenly ardent in her appreciation of classical music. I was just a girl, though older than my years in point of knowledge known and seeings of the spirit. Only I had it at my fingertips. I had it in my bones. Look. (*She shows her hands*) It's not what it looks like, the piano. To the uninitiated the notes look the same. To me, no. Different, all of them. I could tell them in the dark. I could play in the dark, had to sometimes, possibly. And the keys were like rooms. C Major. D Minor. Dark rooms. Light rooms, going up or down a step into another room. It was a mansion to me, music. Heard in the spirit, possibly.

Pause

Only it worried me that playing came easier to me than praying. And I said that, which may have been an error.

Alan Bennett Said it to whom?

Miss Shepherd An ordained priest of great reverence. My confessor. I loved my frocks. Long white arms. People clapping. The flowers brought on. He said that was another vent the devil could creep through. I asked, Was there a middle way? Before I sat down at the keyboard I could possibly say, "I dedicate this performance to God." Or any saint my confessor might choose to nominate. Because it was God-given, I knew that. He said God-given was easily mistaken for devil-sent. So he outlawed the piano. Put paid to music generally. Said that dividends would accrue in terms of growth of the spirit. Which they did. They did. They did. I was good enough to be on the wireless. Earn a living. Offer it to God, Mary. Offer it to God. Cortot. Alfred Cortot. Have you heard of him?

Alan Bennett He was famous.
Miss Shepherd Yes. He was my teacher.

Pause

You play something sometimes that I knew. (*She sings part of the Beethoven Piano Sonata that has been played throughout the play*)

After a bit Alan Bennett joins in and they sing together

How is your mother?
Alan Bennett The same.
Miss Shepherd Still in the coma?
Alan Bennett No.
Miss Shepherd Just having a bit of shut-eye. People do.
Alan Bennett 2 Say good-night.
Alan Bennett Good-night.

Miss Shepherd closes the van door

True to form, she does not reply. There has been some talk about lying. (*He glances at Alan Bennett 2*)

Alan Bennett 2 is a little shame-faced

Still, I do not lie when I say that it was on the morning after Miss Shepherd returned from the day centre, when she lay in the van, her hair washed and braided and between clean sheets, that in that same morning comes the social worker into the garden, bearing clean clothes, linen and ointment, and she knocks on the door of the van.

The Social Worker enters as described

Social Worker Mary. (*She knocks*) Mary? (*She opens the door, looks in and gets into the van*)
Alan Bennett No-one has ever done that before, got into the van.
Alan Bennett 2 She is dead. It is a van no longer. It is a sepulchre.

The Social Worker gets out and Alan Bennett goes and looks in

Even now I do not venture into this evil-smelling tomb but just glimpse her neck stretched out across the new clean pillow as if ready for the block.
Alan Bennett I feel cheated that the discovery of the body has not actually been mine and that, having observed so much for so long, I am not the first to witness her death.

Alan Bennett 2 Now in quick succession come the doctor, the priest and men from the undertaker's, all of whom this bright spring morning do what no-one else has done for twenty years: namely without pause and seemingly without distaste step inside the van.

Pauline and Rufus enter

Pauline Oh, heart.

Alan Bennett 2 Professionals all, I suppose ... one definition of the professional: the absence (or the non-expression) of disgust. (*To Rufus*) Actually you can take this.

Rufus points to himself with a query then goes on with the speech

Rufus Surgeons. Lawyers. Even ... I lower the stakes ... even the gentlemen in brown overalls polishing the faucets in the stalls of the lavatory at the bottom of Parkway. What have they in common? Composure. Control.

Pauline I prefer it when there is *some* feeling.

Rufus No. Be lofty, be sceptical, be serene. By unfeeling we are saved.

Alan Bennett clears out items from the van, holding up the items and almost giving dictation to Alan Bennett 2

Alan Bennett Her Rambo cap. Two bottles of Woodland Glade Moisturizer and After Bath Splash. Many packets of Options, which ought to be a business magazine or a brochure of leisure opportunities but is actually an incontinence pad. Many nasty spotted creeping insects. And a note: "Please arrange funeral", in brackets, "if needed". But no envelope. No next of kin. But there is money. Round her withered neck a bag containing £500. Bank books and building society deposits to the tune of £6,000 and trodden into the layers of sodden, urine-stained newspaper and old clothes that carpet the van there is another £900.

Underwood enters

Underwood She's gone then?

Alan Bennett Yes. On Wednesday.

Underwood Do a bunk, did she?

Alan Bennett In that she died, yes.

Underwood Elbow job, is it? The van?

Alan Bennett Not yet.

Underwood Margaret was very lucky if you ask me. Because they never caught up with her.

Alan Bennett Who?
Underwood The law.
Alan Bennett What had she done?
Underwood It's what she didn't do. A crossroads. Stop. Give way, you know the kind of thing. Major road ahead anyway. Banstead or thereabouts. Our lady at the wheel. Motor bike comes up, too fast maybe. Raining. Brakes, skids, hits the side of the van. Nobody's fault. His, maybe, but not hers. She's stationary at a junction. Gets out. Looks. He's dead. Only young. Dead on the road. Thinks: licence? No. Insurance? No. Sees it all coming. So in a moment of panic — and sin — our holy lady drives off. Skedaddles. Does a bunk. A boy dead on the road and she fucks off. Thereby, you see, committing a felony. And you too, of course. This was an offence. Harbouring a felon.
Alan Bennett What was her real name? Margaret what?

Underwood indicates he wants some money

Of course. That's why you came round. You were blackmailing her?
Underwood I am grieved, sir, that my attempts at elucidation have been so vulgarly misconstrued and since my presence is shortly required in Lisson Grove I will bid you good-afternoon.

Alan Bennett goes back inside the van, looking

Underwood exits

Alan Bennett comes out with an envelope, which he opens

Alan Bennett Fairchild. (*Calling after Underwood*) Was her name Fairchild? Storrington, Sussex?

There is no answer

Leo Fairchild enters the garden

Leo Fairchild Mr Bennett?
Alan Bennett Yes?
Leo Fairchild You've written to me about a Mary Teresa Shepherd, a seventy-nine-year-old woman who has died. I have to tell you I know no such person.
Alan Bennett She names you as her next of kin. She has left some £7,000.
Leo Fairchild It's obviously my sister. Though Shepherd was not her name. She was born Margaret Fairchild. I am Leo Fairchild, her brother. Her

brother who had her put away. In Banstead, which was, of course, an asylum. £7,000!

Alan Bennett Why did you have her put away?

Leo Fairchild God. God, sin, hell. The whole bag of tricks. Morning, noon and night. My poor mother took refuge in the attic. I don't regret it. Though in any case first chance she got she was over the wall and out. And, the important point, stayed free for a year and a day, which meant they couldn't put her back. Odd length of time. A year and a day. Like a fairy story. Well, let me set your mind at rest. I don't want the money. Give it away. Or keep it, why not?

Alan Bennett I couldn't.

Leo Fairchild Think of it as rent. You had her for years. An hour was long enough for me. (*He walks round the van*)

Alan Bennett 2 He's a big disappointment.

Alan Bennett I think he's nice.

Alan Bennett 2 Exactly. Much better for the story if he'd been a money-grabbing shit.

Alan Bennett We could always ... pretend?

Alan Bennett 2 No, we can't. He's still alive.

Leo Fairchild She should have stuck to the piano and maybe none of this would have happened.

Alan Bennett Did she play well?

Leo Fairchild Superbly. Bold and muscular and more like a man would play, I imagine. Great ... dash. No, when she was playing you could forgive Margaret everything.

Music plays; a later movement of the Beethoven piano sonata

Alan Bennett All those years stood on my doorstep she was all the time on the run. Self-sacrifice, incarceration, escape and violent death — A life ... this is what I keep thinking ... a life beside which mine is just dull.

The coffin is carried on by four undertaker's men followed by a priest. They lay it down and it sinks below the level of the stage; the priest blesses and sprinkles the coffin as it goes

Alan Bennett 2 I gaze down on her coffin and reflect that her new quarters are rather more commodious (and certainly sweeter) than that narrow stretch of floor on which she had slept these last twenty years. One of the undertaker's men takes the eye though scarcely more than a boy. Not an occupation one drifts into, I imagine, undertaking, and one that, like becoming a policeman, implies a certain impatience with ordinary slipshod humanity ... and in particular this piece of humanity that has got so slipshod as actually to die. The object of my speculations looks at me briefly and were I Joe Orton, I reflect, I would be able to turn even this bored, impersonal glance across a grave to some sexual advantage. Orton would have found some excuse to absent himself from the graveside a while, have a Jimmy Riddle in the bushes and a quick funereal feel.

Suddenly Miss Shepherd rises from the grave

Miss Shepherd Excuse me, I'm supposed to be the centrepiece here. You should be fighting back the tears, not eyeing up the talent.

Alan Bennett is taken aback

Alan Bennett 2 Well, it's a thought. (*To Miss Shepherd*) What do you think?
Miss Shepherd (*catching sight of Alan Bennett 2*) Oh, hallo. Two of you now. Is that because you're in two minds?
Alan Bennett 2 Yes.
Alan Bennett No.
Miss Shepherd I've been wondering. Would either of you object if the van were to become a place of pilgrimage, possibly?
Alan Bennett 2 No.

They should probably be on either side of her

Alan Bennett I'm getting rid of the van. The van is going.
Miss Shepherd I am thinking of the car that Catholic priest was murdered in in Poland. That became a place of pilgrimage.
Alan Bennett 2 It did, yes.
Alan Bennett Yes. Only you haven't been murdered.
Miss Shepherd (*playing them off against each other*) I haven't been murdered strictly speaking, but I have gone through so much deprivation and want of necessities over a prolonged period, I would have been overjoyed if I had been murdered sometimes.
Alan Bennett 2 Quite.
Miss Shepherd Say the van were left on site, that would encourage a cult. Healing might take place and any proceeds ... donations, jewellery and so forth ... could go towards the nuns.
Alan Bennett The nuns! What did the nuns ever do for you?
Miss Shepherd Not much, but you could take a coals of fire view of it — When the donations start rolling in they'll realize what a catch I would have been. Of course, it was the same with St Bernadette. They only realized with her when it was too late. That's one of the drawbacks of sanctity, that it's generally posthumous. (*To Alan Bennett 2*) That's something you

could do. This play you're writing, pump it up a bit. If it were along the lines of *The Song of Bernadette* it would make you a packet.

Alan Bennett *The Song of Bernadette?*

Miss Shepherd Do you know what your trouble is? Too many scruples in the way. It's always been no all along the line. I've had a much more adventurous life than you, because I got on with it. You, you just sit there. You want to take a leaf out of my book. Be bold.

Alan Bennett 2 How?

Miss Shepherd Why do you just let me die? I'd like to go up into heaven. An ascension. A transfiguration, possibly.

Alan Bennett 2 That's not really my kind of play.

Miss Shepherd Oh, don't you start. You're both as bad as one another. Why not try it, for a change? I came into the garden for three months and stayed for fifteen years. (*She laughs*) Mr Bennett.

Alan Bennett (*both*) Yes.

Miss Shepherd Do you know what that is?

Alan Bennett (*both*) No.

Miss Shepherd It's the last laugh. (*Still laughing, she gets into the van*)

Workmen in hard hats now come on and with a good deal of "All right your end?'-type dialogue which I shan't attempt to transcribe, they attach cables to the van, a flashing orange light off stage indicating the presence of the council truck. Slowly the van is hoisted up and as it ascends the workmen remove their hats, gazing upwards in reverence as, to celestial music and even a heavenly choir, the van disappears from view, leaving the stage dark and desolate and the two Alan Bennetts alone

(*NB That is ideally what should happen and what happened (more or less) on stage in the London version. However, I realize that the resources of the average drama group do not always run to vehicle-lifting gear so you must use the imagination! Try and get the van off the stage as ceremoniously as possible, pushed by the council workers in their hard hats with Miss Shepherd herself perhaps hoisted in her wheelchair to heaven. Something spectacular-ish, anyway, and with lots of music. Good luck!*)

Alan Bennett 2 Starting out as someone incidental to my life, she remained on the edge of it so long she became not incidental to it at all. As homebound sons and daughter looking after their parents think of it as just marking time before their lives start, so like them I learned there is no such thing as marking time, and that time marks you. In accommodating her and accommodating to her, I find twenty years of my life has gone. This broken-down old woman, her delusions and the slow abridgement of her life with all its vehicular permutations — these have been given me to record as others record journeys across Tibet or Patagonia or the thighs of a dozen women. Actually her only permanent legacy is moths — or moth, as the upper classes say. Moths, which I thought went out with my childhood, Mr Attlee, utility furniture and Cremola pudding, now infest my home and the houses of all my neighbours, their eggs like a smudge on the fabric, clustered on the edge of the papers that I sift through for this play.

Alan Bennett I suppose I'm in it?

Alan Bennett 2 Well, what do you think?

They head off

Alan Bennett (*breaking back to address the audience*) Look. This has been one path through my life ... me and Miss Shepherd. Just one track. I wrote things: people used to come and stay the night, and of both sexes. What I mean to say is, it's not as if it's the whole picture. Lots of other stuff happened. No end of things.

Alan Bennett 2 They know that.

Alan Bennett And that's true. I'm not making it up.

Alan Bennett 2 Of course you're not.

Alan Bennett 2 puts his arm around Alan Bennett and they go off together

CURTAIN

FURNITURE AND PROPERTY LIST

ACT I

On stage: IN DESK AREA R: Desk
Desk chair
Lamp
Easy chair
Record player
Newspaper

IN AREA L: street setting

Off stage: Bag of clothes (**Social Worker**)
Plastic sacks (**Miss Shepherd**)
Wheelbarrow of manure (**Workman**)
Van (**Miss Shepherd**)
Walking stick (**Miss Shepherd**)
Robin Reliant (**Miss Shepherd**)

Personal: **Miss Shepherd**: pamphlet, horn
Alan Bennett: coin

Pauline *exits p. 6*

Set: Chair for **Mam**

The light goes down on **Mam** *p.6*

Strike: Chair

Lighting change p. 9

Set: Garden setting including dustbin

Strike: Street setting

ACT II

On stage: Yellow-painted van. *On it*: odd bits of carpet. *Under it*: bulging plastic bags. *In it*: jar, Rambo cap, two bottles Woodland Glade Moisturizer and After Bath Splash, packets of Options (incontinence pads), note, bag containing £500, bank books and building society deposits, stained newspapers, envelope

Off stage: Car battery (**Miss Shepherd**)
Bicycle (**Alan Bennett**)
Wheelchair with cornflake packet fan (**Miss Shepherd**)
Kitchen gloves and two plastic shopping bags (**Alan Bennett**)
Van with hoist (**Ambulance Man**)
Flowers (**Alan Bennett**)
Coffin (**Undertaker's Men**)
Aspergillum (holy water sprinkler) (**Priest**)
Cables (**Workmen**)

LIGHTING PLOT

Property fittings required: nil
Various settings on an open stage

ACT I

To open: Forestage and window inset lit

Cue 1	Front cloth rises *Bring up general lighting over whole stage*	(Page 1)
Cue 2	**Miss Shepherd**: " ... a cheesy smell, possibly." *Fade lights on* **Miss Shepherd**	(Page 2)
Cue 3	**Mam**: "She does it in her britches." *Change to outdoor setting with desk area still lit*	(Page 2)
Cue 4	**Rufus**: " ... this is a community." *Cross-fade to street setting with desk area still lit*	(Page 4)
Cue 5	**Alan Bennett 2**: "It might come in handy." *Fade lights on street setting*	(Page 5)
Cue 6	**Mam** enters L and sits *Bring up light on* **Mam**	(Page 6)
Cue 7	Sound of van starting up *Fade light on* **Mam**	(Page 6)
Cue 8	**Alan Bennett 2**: "' ... a sick woman, dying possibly.'" *Cross-fade to street*	(Page 7)
Cue 9	**Rufus**: "Pinter." *Cross-fade back to desk area*	(Page 8)
Cue 10	**Alan Bennett 2**: " ... on the Everest principle. She's there." *Change to garden setting*	(Page 9)
Cue 11	**Alan Bennett 2**: " ... my bread and butter." *Fade to night-time setting*	(Page 12)

Cue 12   **Miss Shepherd**: "You can't make up your mind."   (Page 13)
             Change to daytime setting L

Cue 13   **Alan Bennett 2**: " ... afterwards be released." Pause   (Page 19)
             Dim to night-time setting

Cue 14   **Miss Shepherd**: " ... through ignorance possibly."   (Page 19)
             Bring up lights on van, making it magical and transparent

Cue 15   **Miss Shepherd**: " ... and to amendment."   (Page 19)
             Fade to night-time setting

Cue 16   **Miss Shepherd** raises her stick   (Page 20)
             Dim light on **Miss Shepherd**

Cue 17   **Mam** enters the desk area   (Page 20)
             Bring up light gradually on desk area

Cue 18   **Miss Shepherd**: "... over to biros."   (Page 24)
             Fade to night-time setting

Cue 19   **Alan Bennett 2**: " ... unrelated to the truth."   (Page 25)
             The van's lights come on

Cue 20   **Underwood**: "Still here, I see, lady."   (Page 25)
             Snap off van lights

Cue 21   **Miss Shepherd** kneels in prayer   (Page 29)
             Fade lights

ACT II

To open: General lighting on desk area and garden

Cue 22   **Miss Shepherd**: " ... she might help."   (Page 33)
             Change lights

Cue 23   **Alan Bennett**: " ... a rational human being."   (Page 34)
             Change lights

Cue 24   **Alan Bennett 2**: " ... it seemed she had."   (Page 35)
             Change lights to evening setting with van in darkness

Cue 25   Sirens and sounds of the Blitz   (Page 37)
             Bring up faint light, slowly growing. Bring up glow on
             van with shaft of light on **Miss Shepherd**

Cue 26   **Miss Shepherd**'s prayer turns into a mutter   (Page 38)
                Fade lights inside and outside the van

Cue 27   **Alan Bennett**: "That's what they all say."   (Page 39)
                Change lights to morning setting with van dark

Cue 28   **Miss Shepherd**: "I can tell you."   (Page 40)
                Change lights

Cue 29   **Alan Bennett 2** pushes **Miss Shepherd** off stage   (Page 41)
                Change lights

Cue 30   **Alan Bennett**: "… what they remind me of."   (Page 44)
                Cross-fade to desk area

Cue 31   **Social Worker**:"I'll see about getting a doctor."   (Page 46)
                Bring up lights on the garden

Cue 32   **Alan Bennett** exits   (Page 49)
                Fade to night-time setting

Cue 33   **Miss Shepherd** gets into the van   (Page 56)
                Flashing orange light

Cue 34   As van disappears from view   (Page 56)
                Dim lights to dark, desolate setting;
                  cut flashing orange light

EFFECTS PLOT

ACT I

Cue 1   When CURTAIN rises   (Page 1)
Hymn sung by chorus of young girls

Cue 2   **Alan Bennett 2** disappears from view   (Page 1)
Abruptly cut off singing

Cue 3   **Alan Bennett**: "We're on the hospital trail again."   (Page 6)
Sound of van starting up

Cue 4   The Lights change to garden setting   (Page 9)
Sound of banging on the side of the van

Cue 5   The Lights fade to night-time setting   (Page 12)
Sound of breaking glass

Cue 6   **Alan Bennett 2**: " ... the effect of each brush stroke."   (Page 15)
Beethoven's Piano Sonata No. 27, Opus 90, in E minor,
plays as if from record player in desk area

Cue 7   **Alan Bennett** switches the music off   (Page 15)
Cut music

Cue 8   **Miss Shepherd** returns to the van   (Page 24)
Beethoven music plays, quietly, as if from record player

Cue 9   **Alan Bennett** puts some piano music on   (Page 27)
Beethoven music as if from record player

Cue 10   **Alan Bennett** turns the music up   (Page 27)
Increase volume of music

Cue 11   **Alan Bennett** turns the music down   (Page 28)
Decrease volume of music; fade under following dialogue

Cue 12   **Miss Shepherd**: "I tried it and it was open."   (Page 28)
Beethoven music plays — as if played on a very poor piano

Cue 13   **Alan Bennett**: "... just after the war."   (Page 28)
             Fade poor piano music and bring up the conclusion
             of a spectacular piano piece; at its end, a wave of applause

Cue 14   **Miss Shepherd** sinks into an awkward curtsy   (Page 29)
             Cut applause

ACT II

Cue 15   The **Social Worker** exits   (Page 34)
             Sound of Robin Reliant being revved

Cue 16   **Alan Bennett 2**: " ... the papers from the doormat." (Page 34)
             Revving slows down and stops

Cue 17   **Alan Bennett 2**: " ... Miss Shepherd's plastic bags." (Page 34)
             Miss Shepherd tries and fails to start the car

Cue 18   **Alan Bennett 2**: "The time of her life."   (Page 37)
             Distant sirens, sound of the Blitz, then fade

Cue 19   **Leo Fairchild**: " ... forgive Margaret everything."   (Page 54)
             Music; a later movement of the Beethoven piano sonata

Cue 20   The van is hoisted up   (Page 56)
             Celestial music with heavenly choir